Praise for *Family Tales, Family Wisdom*

"A blueprint for reconstructing life stories into vivid historical memoir . . . filled with provocative and poignant insights about the nature of memories, how to inspire them, and how to gather and preserve them."   —*The Boston Globe*

"Here's the answer to the generation gap. A beautiful and inspiring book that will open up new channels of caring and understanding among all family members. A gift of love."
          —Elaine Mazlish, coauthor of *How to Talk So Kids Will Listen/Listen So Kids Will Talk*

"Harvesting family history, talking 'bout generations, Robert U. Akeret gives a blueprint for families to follow in compiling elder tales."   —*The Washington Post*

"A moving and illuminating book that promotes the understanding of one's history and the healing of family wounds. Dr. Akeret has paved the way for a new movement: the return to our roots."—Victoria Secunda, author of *When You and Your Mother Can't Be Friends*

"The book tells you how to get mom and dad and grandma and grandpa to tell the stories of their lives. You may find pearls of wisdom. Catch them while you can."
          —*The Charlotte Observer*

"Fascinating . . . This book comes at a time when families are concerned about their roots . . . and there is a treasure there."
          —Larry Freund, "Voice of America"

"Post-eighties America needs to hear its family stories. Use your stories to help restore values that have been lost over the years."   —*Chicago Tribune*

Family Tales,
Family Wisdom

OTHER BOOKS BY ROBERT U. AKERET, ED.D.

Photoanalysis
Not by Words Alone

Family Tales, Family Wisdom

How to Gather the Stories of a Lifetime and Share Them with Your Family

Robert U. Akeret, Ed.D.

with
Daniel Klein

An Owl Book
Henry Holt and Company
New York

To Our Families—
Past, Present, and Future

Copyright © 1991 by Robert Akeret and Daniel Klein
All rights reserved, including the right to reproduce
this book or portions thereof in any form.
Published by Henry Holt and Company, Inc.,
115 West 18th Street, New York, New York 10011.
Published in Canada by Fitzhenry & Whiteside Limited,
91 Granton Drive, Richmond Hill, Ontario L4B 2N5.

Library of Congress Cataloging-in-Publication Data
Akeret, Robert U.
Family tales, family wisdom: how to gather the stories of a
lifetime and share them with your family / Robert U. Akeret with
Daniel Klein.—1st Owl book ed.
p.   cm.
Originally published: New York: Morrow, © 1991.
Includes bibliographical references.
1. Reminiscing in old age. 2. Aged—Psychology. 3. Psychology—
Biographical methods. I. Klein, Daniel M. II. Title.
[BF724.85.R45A44   1992]
306.87—dc20   92-18866
                                                              CIP

ISBN 0-8050-2311-9 (An Owl Book: pbk.)

Henry Holt books are available at special discounts
for bulk purchases for sales promotions, premiums,
fund-raising, or educational use. Special editions
or book excerpts can also be created to specification.

For details contact: Special Sales Director,
Henry Holt and Company, Inc., 115 West 18th Street,
New York, New York 10011.

First published in hardcover by
William Morrow and Company in 1991.

First Owl Book Edition—1992

Designed by Paul Bacon Studio Inc.
Printed in the United States of America
Recognizing the importance of preserving
the written word, Henry Holt and Company, Inc.,
by policy, prints all of its first editions
on acid-free paper. ∞

1   3   5   7   9   10   8   6   4   2

Photograph credits appear on page 235.

Acknowledgments

We want to express our great appreciation to all the families who participated so generously and so enthusiastically in the development of the Elder Tale Program. They asked the questions never asked and told the stories never told, and in so doing reinvented the Elder Tale ritual.

We also want to thank Dan's wife, Freke Vuijst, for her careful reading of the early drafts of the manuscript, Robi's good friend, Paul Bacon, for his cover and design of the book, and our agent, Howard Morhaim, and our editor, Liza Dawson, for their abiding faith in this project.

Finally, we want to thank Robi's family—his mother, Emmi, his wife, Ann, his daughters Kim, Julie, Liza, and Teal, his sons-in-law Tony and John, and his grandchildren Molly, Nicky, and Will, for they provided the seed experience that inspired this reinvention of the Elder Tale ritual.

—R. U. A.
Grog Harbor
Essex, N.Y.

—D. M. K.
Great Barrington, Mass.

Contents

INTRODUCTION: *The Story Begins. . . .*

I've never met a person of any age who didn't want to know more about his parents' and grandparents' lives.

What were they like as children? How did it feel growing up in their family? In their neighborhood? In their country? Who were their friends? Whom did they love? What were their dreams? Their fears? The turning points of their lives? What were the events and experiences that shaped them?

And a thousand other questions.

Wanting to understand who our parents and grandparents really are, wanting to grasp the whole sweep of their lives—from childhood to old age—is a fundamental curiosity. And for very good reason. Because we know intuitively that what shaped their lives has shaped our lives too. We know their stories are finally our own stories, and that hearing those stories can ultimately link us to the history of mankind.

Yet somehow most of our questions go unasked, and most of their stories go untold. And then the day comes when our parents and grandparents are gone, and their stories—that link—are gone with them.

I remember rushing to see my father as he lay dying in a Lucerne hospital. On the flight over to Switzerland, my mind was flooded with questions I'd always wanted to ask him. What had his years in South Africa been like? Why had he slept with a pistol under his pillow when he was living in Bucharest? Had he loved my mother very much before their marriage broke apart? When I reached my father's side, all he could say was a final "Bravo, Robi!" before he slipped away. My unasked questions went unanswered, and they continued to plague me for months after his funeral. Where had his love for exotic plants come from? Had he fought with his parents before he left home? Friends and colleagues assured me that my preoccupation with these unasked questions was a "natural" part of mourning, yet that explanation did nothing to assuage the feelings of incompleteness and disconnectedness that I was experiencing.

It took my own children—and grandchildren—to help me begin to make sense of those feelings many years later. And when that happened, they set me off on one of the greatest personal and professional adventures of my life.

More than a decade after my father's death, my eldest daughter, Kim, approached me with a plan she had devised for the upcoming summer. When my eighty-five-year-old mother, Emmi, came over from Switzerland for her annual stay with us at our family retreat on Lake Champlain, Kim wanted to make a video of Emmi reminiscing through her life. Kim said she wanted to do this as much for her own children as for herself. She asked for my blessing and my help.

I hesitated. Is this the way I wanted to spend a big chunk of my cherished summer vacation? Would it really be such a good idea to put my mother through this? Couldn't it unleash all kinds of messy emotions? Mightn't it feel to her as if she were delivering her last testament—a prelude to her death? And how would this project affect the rest of our family? My wife, Ann, already suffered some resentment of my mother's incursions on our summers. Wouldn't devoting a week—perhaps several—to making a movie starring my mother be more than any wife could be expected to bear?

As these objections clicked through my mind, my Kimmie smiled at me with her big hazel eyes as if she could read my thoughts.

"It's just that I have all these questions that I've always wanted to ask Granny," my daughter said quietly.

Unasked questions.

"Maybe this is something the whole family could do together," I replied, smiling back.

Thus began my first family experience with Elder Tales. At that time, I was barely aware of the fact that Elder Tale—Telling had a long tradition in a large variety of cultures and that only relatively recently that tradition had slipped away from ours. Yet instinctively, all of us in my family went about setting up these memoir sessions with my mother as if we were re-creating a lost ritual. What we were doing felt natural, even familiar, as though we knew in our bones that this was something families once did together as a normal way of linking one generation to another.

Ireland—
Bernie

But, of course, we were improvising as we went along. From my experience with photoanalysis, I knew that family photographs were a powerful key to retrieving memories—not merely the events, people, and locales of our past, but the feelings attached to these memories. I knew that one highly charged photo could set off a chain of a dozen or more personal stories. So I asked my mother to search through her photo albums and sift through her shoeboxes of loose photos for the ones that seemed the most evocative to her. Similarly, Kim asked her to bring along any scrapbooks, journals, saved letters, and news clippings she thought might help her recall her life stories. My second daughter, Julie, suggested that Granny select any small mementos or souvenirs that held special meaning for her—a piece of jewelry, a ticket stub, a menu. And my granddaughter, Molly, wanted Emmi to bring along her traditional Zurich folk costume. When my mother arrived at the airport that summer, she had brought one more suitcase than usual—a particularly heavy one!

"I've got a museum in there," she laughed, as I struggled to lift it.

Our project didn't always go smoothly. None of us knew where or how to begin. And once we finally got going, we weren't sure how to progress: How could we help Emmi move toward the most significant stories of her life? Were there different ways she could convey her stories to us? And how could we keep this whole process playful and unselfconscious while at the same time giving it the weight and respect of an important family ritual? We didn't find completely satisfying answers to most of these programmatic questions that summer.

It ultimately took years of working with a variety of families to develop and refine the Elder Tale Program that I am able to offer in this book. But what *did* happen that summer touched all of us in my family very deeply. Yes, some tears were shed (most of them at surprising moments), and a few times we laughed so hard and so long that some videotapes recorded nothing but open mouths and the sound of laughter. But most of the time we were simply and quietly entranced by the spectacle of the stories of an entire lifetime spinning out before us, stories that connected all of us, all four generations in that summer house.

And in remarkable ways, those feelings lingered with us long after that summer was over. Miraculously, tensions between my wife and my mother began to evaporate, gradually replaced by renewed mutual respect and affection; and this, in turn, allowed me to enjoy my mother's company in ways I hadn't been able to in years. My granddaughter, Molly, after having listened spellbound to my mother's adventures in the theater world of Vienna, declared that fall that she, too, wanted to become an actress, and asked to take voice lessons. And my mother, who had seemed to us increasingly withdrawn over the last few years, now appeared more energized and engaged in the world. Even her walk changed from hesitant, mincing steps to a stronger, more confident gait.

"I am feeling very happy about the time we had this summer," she wrote to all of us from Switzerland. "We built some bridges together, didn't we?"

Clearly, something powerful had happened to us all.

That fall, I found myself listening to my patients in a different way. I was suddenly aware of the gnawing guilt and sense of helplessness so many of them felt about their aging parents. It seemed every Monday several patients would report a disastrous weekend visit with the "old folks." Their parents either had had nothing to say to them or they had said the same things over and over again. Many had complained about their health and future prospects, while others had talked endlessly about friends who had died. It was clear that most of them were battling feelings of despair and an eroding sense of dignity. Their children and grandchildren usually returned home from these visits thoroughly depressed and exhausted.

There was one forty-two-year-old woman who said to me unhappily:

"We've tried everything to bring some pleasure into my parents' lives, but nothing clicks. Of course, it's not simply pleasure they want—it's purpose, it's meaning. But how in the world can I give them that?"

"Maybe there is a way," I answered.

So, for the first time, I introduced the idea of Elder Tale–Telling to another family.

Then, one by one, I introduced it to more families. And as I worked with them, I gradually began to discover a variety of ways to make the experience richer, to make it both more playful and more profound.

I ventured into all of this hoping it would create new connections between generations, but I never could have anticipated how much spontaneous healing would occur between them. Listeners came away from these experiences with a new awareness of their parents (and grandparents). Many spoke of being deeply moved in a way similar to how they felt after reading an important book. And hardly a session passed without somebody saying in utter amazement, "I can't believe I never knew that about you!" They were suddenly seeing a parent or grandparent as an individual with a life and subjectivity of his own; and with this perception came renewed respect for the elder as well as a deeper understanding of themselves.

When I started, I was drawn to Elder Tale–Telling by its value to the listener, but soon I found myself thinking more and more about the tale's value to the teller. I was aware, of course, of special programs in church groups and nursing homes where social workers came to record oral histories, yet I wondered if this approach went far and deep enough. One day, not long after I began introducing Elder Tales to other families, I impulsively went to my file cabinet and looked back almost ten years to a case that had been flickering somewhere deep in my memory, the case of a man I'll call George.

George had been referred to me by my teacher and colleague Rollo May. When George called to make his first appointment, I'd noticed that his voice had some of the creaks and whistles of age, but thought little of it until he walked into my office ten days later, and I saw a man who looked a good eighty years old. Indeed, George turned out to be eighty-nine!

I was just fifty at the time, and thus far in my practice had never worked with anyone over sixty-five, let alone someone almost ninety. Most of the adults who sought my help had been young or middle-aged men and women, people still in their generative years, who wanted, in some very broad sense, to make changes in the way they lived the rest of their lives. But what changes could a retired eighty-nine-year-old widower be aspiring to?

When I asked George why he had come to see me, he fumpferred around for several minutes before saying, "I just don't feel connected to the world anymore."

"Not even to your children?"

"Not to my *life*," he replied.

I was intrigued.

"Well, why don't you tell me a little about this life you don't feel connected to," I said.

George hesitated for several minutes, scratching his craggy head and peering around my office. Then he cleared his throat and began, "Well, there was that time back in '31 when the Bonus Marchers came into town. I was living in Cincinnati—out of work like everybody else—so I decided to march along with them for a few days. . . ."

By the hour's end, George had recounted this and several other vivid and colorful slices of his life. But why he had told them and what they revealed about his "problem" escaped me.

At the beginning of our next session, without any urging, George launched into another story from his past—this one about a practical joke he and some school friends had pulled on a gym teacher. It was a good story, and I told him so. George smiled and followed it immediately with another, about the time he'd bought a dozen roses for his piano teacher but once inside her apartment had been too embarrassed to give them to her, so had tossed them out her open window into the back of a horse-drawn milk wagon.

I had already abandoned the idea of looking for traditional psychoanalytic interpretations of the material George was giving me. After all, our goal at this point in his life obviously was not going to be an analysis of the early formation of his personality in an attempt to change it now. Yet my instincts told me that there was some way I could be of use to George. When I saw how much livelier he had become by the end of that session—his eyes brighter and his gestures sharper—I decided to let his stories keep rolling for a while.

Roll they did. For the next several months, George told me one tale after another from various stages of his life— from his childhood and adolescence, from his young adulthood and middle age. This man had a thousand wonderful stories to tell. As I listened, I found myself revising a number of myths I'd been carrying around about older people. George, on the brink of ninety, wasn't at all preoccupied with death. His memory, especially of the distant past, was fabulous, and his wit intact. And, although he'd come into my office disturbed by a feeling of disconnectedness, I could hardly describe him as depressed. George's "problem," it seemed to me, was finding what he could do meaningfully at this stage of his life.

And after a while I did figure out how I could be of use to him: I could help him link his stories together, help him pick up the themes that threaded through his life and identify what we call in German his *lebenslauf*, the sweep of his life. In short, I could help him look back over his life and try to make sense of it.

For example, after hearing George tell one particular

story, I said to him, "You seem to have gotten most of what you wanted in life through sheer instinct and good luck, rather than by careful planning. Lucky you! You remind me of Zeno in the novel *The Confessions of Zeno*. Zeno had a brother-in-law who played the stock market by studying graphs, but Zeno played it by closing his eyes and wishing his stocks up—and somehow he always came out ahead. It's a wonderful book."

At our next session, George told me that he had read the novel I'd mentioned, and indeed he did see parallels— many of them comic—between its main character's life and his own. He grinned and told me some other stories that picked up the "Zeno" theme in his own life.

About eight months after he first came into my office, George announced to me that he was moving to Santa Fe, not far from his daughter and grandchildren, and that this would be his last session. I had watched George grow progressively more animated as this storytelling process miraculously "reconnected" him to his life. Now I imagined him continuing to tell his stories to his daughter and grandchildren.

Just before he left, I asked George to describe what he felt he had accomplished with me.

"That's easy, Robert," George replied with a wry smile. "Thanks to you, I think I've finally got my story straight."

How could I have nearly forgotten the power of George's desire to tell his life stories? Or the profound satisfaction he'd taken in detecting their themes? Recalling my experience with George, I saw clearly that the Elder Tale Program had to be as much about never-told stories as about never-asked questions.

Now, in addition to looking for ways to stimulate the tale-teller's memory, I began searching out ways for him to recognize his core life stories and to uncover the themes that link these stories together. I was creating a program for someone to look back over a long life and try to make sense of it—a way for a person to get his story straight.

To this end, I went back to some of my original work in photoanalysis—analyzing family photographs for hidden meanings—looking for ways that photoanalysis could provide a tale-teller with clues to the critical junctures in his life. I looked for clues in films and literature. And, drawing from a variety of sources, I developed some ideas for interpreting the special, often spectacular, dreams that come to a person as he becomes involved in putting together his life story.

For me—a man in his sixties—this became the most exciting part of the program. It became especially satisfying when tale-tellers began reporting to me that by using these tools and resources, they were experiencing the sweet magic of insight. Every once in a while they would come upon an image or dream sequence, a link between their stories or a parallel between their own story and one in a book or movie that seemed to say, "Yes! That's what my life's been all about!"

But always my hardest job is getting families started.

Everybody assures me that they are genuinely curious about their parents' and grandparents' lives, but somehow they manage to come up with a hundred and one excuses for not sitting down to listen to their stories. I can hardly fault them—I remember all too clearly my own resistance when my daughter first suggested we make a project of getting my own mother's stories. And elders are no different; although they tell me they yearn for better contact with their children and grandchildren, they also come up with a hundred and one excuses for not telling their stories.

I can understand them very well too. I had to confront one of my own basic resistances soon after I began working on the Elder Tale Program when a woman in her forties asked me ingenuously, "Do you think of yourself as an elder, Dr. Akeret?"

I swallowed hard.

Me, an elder? With my mother still living? No siree. Not yet. I mean, sure, I'm a grandfather in my sixties, but, hey—

And then I realized that my reflexive response was the same as most elders—embarrassment at my age, fear at being taken as "over the hill," everything but proud of my status as a possessor of stories and wisdom.

"Of course I'm an elder," I answered finally.

From then on, that honorable title sprang to my lips automatically.

Resistances to the Elder Tale Program take a variety of forms, ranging from elders who complain, "I'm too old to start analyzing myself!" to children who protest, "Isn't this like asking my father to write his own epitaph?" Later in this book, I'll devote more time to addressing these many resistances; for now, let me say that most of them seem to fall into two general categories: the fear of boring stories and the fear of "dangerous" stories.

Elders frequently argue that they think their lives are too trivial and boring to merit all the "fuss" of the Elder Tale Program.

"Who am I? George Washington? General MacArthur? Kirk Douglas?" one old man said to his daughter when she broached the idea to him. "Memoirs are for big shots, not for me."

"But *you* are my father, and Kirk Douglas isn't!" the daughter retorted. "I want to know *your* story!"

Of course she does. Why do so many elders find this hard to believe? Are they so bamboozled by the ridiculous idea that a life story worth telling has to begin and end with great public achievements and honors? Or, at the very least, that it has to be full of fabulous, movielike adventures? These people simply don't understand that their own stories, the personal dramas that give the feel of the times and places they have passed through, are the stories their children and grandchildren want to hear.

But even more important, these elders fail to grasp *how inherently fascinating their lives actually have been*. To paraphrase Flaubert, every life is worthy of a novel—especially a long life. Happily, once elders begin digging out their stories, they invariably start to discover how remarkably interesting their lives have been. And that discovery can be incredibly invigorating. Suddenly, elders who had closed themselves off with feelings of insignificance found their daily perceptions becoming richer, their thinking more acute, and most important, their zest for living growing in leaps and bounds. Their stories had confirmed the significance of their lives. Now, instead of receding from life, they embraced it.

On the other side of the family, there are many children and grandchildren who tell me they are afraid they'll be bored by listening to Elder Tales. They imagine the old folks rambling on tediously for hours, wasting their time.

I assure these people that in the program we've worked out, no listener can escape being interested, and in any event, Tale-Telling sessions rarely go on much longer than an hour—the length of an average television drama. And while it's true that their parents' or grandparents' stories won't have the production values of a multimillion-dollar television drama, what it will have is *immediacy and personal relevance and genuine feeling*.

And *that*, I suspect, is what this line of resistance is actually all about—the dread of feeling *too much*, not of feeling too little.

It's an understandable fear. Feelings *will* flow in these sessions, laughter and tears—the whole works. Perhaps not during the telling of the first few stories, but as the elder begins to reveal more and more about herself, uncovers and tells the core stories of her life, takes you through the high points, low points, and turning points of her life, you can be assured no one involved will go untouched.

But not bored. Not by a long shot.

Telling Elder Tales makes lives real. It makes everyone involved aware of the cycle of life in a way few experiences can. The feelings generated by that experience are of a whole different order from the feelings we squeak out while watching even the most sophisticated movie about people we don't know.

And so we come to the fear of feeling "too much," of cans of worms irreversibly opening and emotions somehow getting out of control and becoming dangerous in these sessions. My experience with Elder Tale–Telling is that that simply doesn't happen. The program is constructed in such a way that families come to emotional material by degrees—and only when everyone is well prepared. Nothing's forced. Any family member can blow the whistle if she feels a story is dangerous, that it is going in a direction that feels too emotionally risky to her. No secrets are told against anyone's wishes. This is not family therapy that we are doing here—it's remarkably therapeutic, but it's not therapy.

"But what do we need a program for anyway?" people often ask me. "It seems so artificial, so contrived. Isn't there a simpler and more natural way to get the same thing going?"

There once was. As we'll discuss in the next chapter, telling Elder Tales was once a normal part of life in many societies. But, for a variety of reasons, that tradition has mostly vanished, and so, yes, it does take something deliberate, something planned, to get this tradition started again for us today.

Dozens of people have told me about the time they gave their parents a family tree or a scrapbook or a photo album to fill in with their personal histories, but nothing came of it. The parents promised to get to work on it soon, but months, then years, slipped by, and nothing happened. From this experience, the children concluded that their parents were unwilling—or maybe even unable—to produce some kind of life history for their heirs.

But what could they reasonably expect their parents to produce in isolation? A blank page is intimidating to most of us. Where to begin? What to include? *And what for, anyhow?*

What I offer here is as much a "reason-to-do" and "getting-to-do" book as it is a "how-to-do" book. And although it will certainly help people produce memoir documents in the form of scrapbooks and albums, audiotapes and videotapes, our primary purpose is to generate powerful experiences, not just documents. And these experiences culminate in the telling of the tales—a communal act—re-creating a family ritual.

I've divided the book into three parts:

Part I, "Remember When Old Used to Mean Wise?,"

explores the Elder Tale tradition in other cultures and why it's slipped away from ours, then looks into the elder's unique capabilities of mind and perspective as a storyteller and conveyor of wisdom.

Part II, "Discovering the Hero of Your Life," offers the resources and tools for triggering your stories, shaping them, and finding the themes that connect them, ranging from photoanalysis to a method for decoding "life-story" dreams.

Part III, "The Elder Tale Program," outlines the ten-step program itself, starting with freewheeling "Snapshot" anecdotes of childhood and working up to "Sentimental Journeys"—storytelling trips to landmarks of the past—and finally to core "Stories I Never Told."

Throughout all three parts, I'll be sharing scores of Elder Tales, along with experiences of the people who told them and the people who listened to them, showing how these tales weave families together—resolving the mysteries of untold stories and opening hearts.

In a sense, all I have done here is to provide a framework for a natural desire, a "kit," and a rationale for a life-cycle process that once occurred as part of the cultural course of things. I've tried my best to put this together in an entertaining form, accessible to both older readers and their children and grandchildren, for above all what I hope to provide is a ritual that reconnects one generation to another.

"Memoir," a writer once said, "is how we validate our lives."

It is also an act of love.

"Wisdom springs from life experience well-digested."

—ERIK ERIKSON

PART I

Remember When Old Used to Mean Wise?

"When a knowledgeable old person dies, a whole library disappears."
                                                    —African proverb

"My grandmother'd tell us things about the Depression. You can read about it, too. What they tell us is different than what you read."
                        —LILY IN *Hard Times: An Oral History of the Great Depression*

CHAPTER 1 *Running Out of Wisdom*

———

It's hard to imagine that in other cultures and at earlier times in our own culture, people actually looked forward to growing old. For them, old age was life's crowning stage, the best of life for which the first was made. In their myths and in their daily lives, the elders were considered blessed with unique knowledge and special powers. They were honored and revered. Old meant wise.

But not in America. And certainly not today.

I'd be hard-pressed to find many people in our country who actually look forward to growing old. Most expect only to lose powers, not to gain them—at least not to gain powers that are considered useful. Without useful powers, they anticipate gradually losing the respect of their families and communities. And without respect, they can look forward to losing their sense of dignity.

But it was not always so—nor is it everywhere so, as I began to appreciate as I dug deeper into this subject. Reading about elders in other times and in other places, I realized that a great number of our society's ideas and expectations about old age are not givens—they are not chiseled in stone. What "old age" means and how we experience it turns out to be as much a function of cultural myths and values as of the biology of aging. Thinking about this, I began to gradually gain faith that we, like one remarkable American Indian tribe I came across in my reading, could actually begin to reinvent old age for ourselves. And a giant step toward that goal would be to rediscover the wisdom inherent to elders.

Almonds and Wisdom

I remember once, as a young man traveling on my own in Spain, stopping at a café in a small mountain village and suddenly hearing a medley of voices singing a lilting song. I looked up and saw a beautiful group of villagers, a mix of young children and elders, most of whom looked to be in their seventies and eighties, walking slowly up a stony path with empty hemp sacks slung over their shoulders. I asked the waiter where they were going.

"To gather almonds," he answered. "It is their work."

"The young and the old together?"

"Yes, they are well matched," he told me. "The children climb the trees and shake the almonds out, then climb down and gather them up. And the old sit under the trees holding the almond sacks open in their laps and telling the children stories."

How very well matched indeed.

In a great many "unsophisticated" and primitive societies, the elders spend much of their time with youngsters, minding, entertaining, and teaching them while the children's parents engage in more physically demanding work. It is a good deal for everybody. In these societies, it seems self-evident to everyone that their eldest members are their wisest and best teachers—after all, they've had a longer time to learn how things are done and what things mean. The elders are, in a way, the sum of the culture's history—the last word on why things are the way they are. Passing their knowledge on to the young is, more than anything, what gives the culture continuity, the glue that holds it together. And so, as teachers and storytellers, the elders are highly valued in these "simple" societies.

I'm thinking, for example, of the Kirghiz people of Afghanistan, a small group of herders who revere their elders, especially for their knowledge of tribal history and lore. This people's principal storytellers, known as *erchi*, are usually at least seventy years old. They sing epic songs that can go on for hours as they unfold mythic tales about gold-capped mountains and talking birds, evil-spirited snakes and two-fisted heroes. Through story and symbol, these songs tell what is valued in their culture, what is beautiful, and what is meaningful. To while away a long winter night, the *erchi* will also sing personal songs they have composed about the life and adventures of an ancestor or about significant events in their own lives. These musical Elder Tales recount heroic triumphs and painful defeats, bawdy encounters and happy courtships, family feuds and comic misunderstandings. Through the experiences and character of the tale-teller and his forebears, the songs tell how this family came to be the way it is. The songs convey how the new generations are connected to the past and how, ultimately, they all fit into the life cycle.

For the Kirghiz children, grandchildren, and great-grandchildren listening around the fire, these songs bear wisdom. Although their elders also provide them with practical information—for example, veterinary and midwifery techniques—it is for their mythic lore and family histories that they are most valued. They offer what we, in our culture, call a philosophical or literary perspective: a look at life's mysteries and options, its conflicts and comforts. They provide maps of the cultural landscape: ways to live.

Of course, the Kirghiz elders suffer the same physical deterioration we all do; in fact, they are particularly prone to blindness in old age. But they do not consider the physical deficiencies of aging to be indignities. As long as they have their voices, they participate fully and proudly in family and tribal affairs. And although they may complain of occasional lapses of memory, there is no concept of "senility" in the Kirghiz language. In this culture, growing old is purely and simply a process of growing wise: As long as the elders have stories to tell—or to sing—they are revered and cherished as the wisest of their people.

The tradition of elders as wise men and women can be found in primitive societies on every continent. Among the !Kung of Africa, a group of hunter-gatherers in the Kalahari Desert, the elders are prized for their knowledge of kinship systems and secret initiation rites as well as for tribal histories and family stories. In !Kung society, the old are literally considered the "creators" of the next generation of mature, productive tribe members. Among the Hindus of the small south Indian hamlets, elders devote themselves to spiritual pursuits and become the village sages who interpret moral and spiritual issues for the rest of the community. And on and on. From islanders in Micronesia to Bolivian mountain people, old means wise.

There are exceptions, of course—those primitive societies that have always considered their elders more of an economic burden than a cultural treasure. We've all heard, for example, of how the Eskimos sent their old out into the cold to perish once they'd outlived their usefulness. But from what I've learned, that's not the way things usually happen. The more common scenario is of a primitive society that at first reveres its old and cherishes their wisdom, but then turns away from them after it comes in contact with a more "sophisticated" culture. It seems that one of the ways that we, in the modern world, have "enlightened" primitive societies is by leading them to abandon the wisdom of their elders.

I'm thinking, for example, of the Asmat people of Indonesian New Guinea. In their "precontact" days as headhunters and raiders, these people completely venerated their oldest members. In their mythology, the highest deity was known as "the Oldest Man." For them, old age equaled knowledge and experience. Even when the Asmat elders weakened physically, their influence was not diminished, because they increased their participation in rituals and in training the young. But as soon as the Asmat aborigines were "pacified" by the Indonesians, their centuries-old ritual system began to fall apart. It was entirely gone—replaced by missionary religions and cargo cults—in a matter of years. And gone with it was a role for their old people. The Asmat elders now live in what anthropologists call a "ritual void." Whereas they once sat at the center of a circle of young men, holding forth on headhunting rites and battle adventures, they now sit alone. No one listens to the Asmat old men anymore.

Well, God knows, I certainly don't approve of head-hunting, yet the fate of the Asmat elders still strikes me as tragic. Tragic and familiar.

And now I'm starting to worry about the Kirghiz elders. A field anthropologist who recently visited these people reported that one particular import from the modern world is beginning to take its toll on their epic singers, the old *erchi*. The transistor radio has arrived, and now some Kirghiz young people would rather listen to Radio Afghanistan than to the songs of their ancestors.

Young Is Wise?

What is it about modern culture that relegates elders to a place outside the circle and away from the fire?

It's not as if the idea of the Wise Old Man (and Woman) is foreign to us. Our own tradition of old as wise dates back to biblical times, to the white-bearded Abraham and Moses, the original learned old rabbis who spoke with the wisdom of the ages. There was a similar tradition in classical Greece. I remember reading Plato for the first time as a college student and being impressed by his argument for why the elders should be the rulers of the Greek city-state: because only the old are enlightened, free, and wise enough to put the community's interest ahead of their own. Old as wise had a place in classical Roman tradition too. Cicero rhapsodized about the glorious transcendent spirit of men and women in the last stage of life, rich in experience and knowledge, qualities that he called the "natural endowment of old age." In old Norse history, elders were the tribal storytellers, the bearers of the oral tradition of sagas. The image of the wise elder—the king's wizened old wizard with his esoteric advice, the bearded high priest with his trenchant philosophies, the "ancient mariner" with his spellbinding tales, the winking old matriarch with her fascinating family stories—persisted in Europe through the centuries. And although at some times and in some regions there was a countertradition of the laughable old fool, there in general remained a respect for the elder as a bearer of folk and

family wisdom. This tradition continued in almond or-
chards, by hearthsides, and at dinner tables, from Malaga
to Marseilles to Cork, up to the beginning of this century.

Just what is it that has gradually been bringing this
tradition to an end?

The majority of social historians I've read put most of
the blame on technology and economics. Once technical
know-how began to change rapidly, the elders ceased to be
society's experts. With the coming of new farming and hus-
bandry methods, new craft and manufacturing techniques,
the oldest members of the community were replaced by
younger women and men as the conveyors of practical information. And once Grandfather and Grandmother were
no longer the last word on how to do things, they quickly
began to lose the general respect of their youngers. In fact,
anything having to do with the "old ways" started to lose
value. If the old folks didn't know the best way to grow,
raise, hunt, or make things, could they possibly know anything about life that was of value?

Parallel to this trend was the democratization and pro-
fessionalization of education. What for centuries had been
learned directly from parents and grandparents was now
learned from professional teachers and from books. Gradually, these specialists were replacing the elders in teaching
everything—not just, say, farming and craft-making, but ultimately history and philosophy as well. The wisdom of the
elders was clearly losing ground.

The tradition of the elder as wiseman, family historian,
folklorist, and storyteller was further eroded by an increase
of mobility, both geographic and social. Think of mass em-
igration to America. Starting with the first settlers, most of
the people who came to the New World were bent on making a clean break from the Old. It was a time for fresh starts,
to put the old ways behind and reinvent oneself from top to
bottom. Over the years, this became central to the American immigrant tradition: Throw off your old clothes, your
old customs, even your old language, and become an American—in effect, become a person without a past. It was an
exhilarating experience.

I had a little insight into this exhilaration during my first crossing of the Atlantic by ship many years ago. Starting at my first shipboard supper, I met one young man and woman after another who had fabulous backgrounds: counts and heiresses, lyric poets and prima ballerinas. It was not until my fourth day at sea that the bursar took me aside and confided to me with a smile that that count over there lounging on the foredeck was in reality a Brooklyn florist, and, yes, that ballerina was a college girl from Boston. "Folks make up wonderful stories about themselves on ships," he told me. "For a few days at sea, there are no relatives or old friends to burden a man with the truth."

The same could be said for many an American immigrant: He could make himself up. Crucial to all social mobility is the ability to dismiss or revise your family history. But when you erase your past—your heritage, your folklore, your family history—you erase your elders as well, because they are the wellspring of your background stories.

In many cases, immigrant elders collaborated in making themselves extinct.

"I wanted my kids to be real Americans," an old Latvian immigrant once told me. "So I never taught them my language, never told them anything about life over there—my people, the way I grew up. I thought it would just confuse them. You know, hold them back."

In the more recent American past, geographic mobility and high technology have dealt what has seemed like the final blow to the tradition of the elder as the repository and teller of family stories. Migration from rural areas to cities and from cities to suburbs has severed generations as radically as transoceanic voyages once did. A suburban neighborhood has virtually no collective past; in suburbia, comfort has supplanted history. And one of those comforts that began appearing inside the new American family's home in the middle of this century was a piece of proactive furniture that could spew forth the stories of strangers at a relentless and dazzling speed—the television set. This technological marvel quickly moved to the center of the family circle; huddled around the TV, the entire family went silent, and many have remained silent ever since. No one's stories can compete with those flashing from the box, least of all an elder's.

As elders recede as a resource in a society, youth inevitably rises as an ideal. Now more than ever, we in America are a youth-centered culture. Not just in our preoccupation with beauty and physical energy, but in the realm of ideas as well. For us, new ideas are by definition better than old ideas. The latest is the best. Old is out-of-date—irrelevant. Now *young* is wise!

In this cultural mind-set, it is normal for a person to aspire desperately to perpetual youth rather than to look forward to growing old. Today, no one wants to grow older than thirty, let alone to grow old. People have begun to recoil from the idea of progressive stages of life. They don't want to be a part of unfolding history. They want to stop the life cycle—and get off.

Little wonder that the elderly suffer from what I call the "bad press syndrome." Our youth-obsessed culture can only conceive of old age as an illness, can only see elders as frail, depressed, and unproductive. And such an assessment all too frequently leads us to think of ourselves this way.

Whatever the sum of forces are that have conspired to make it so, we, along with most of the rest of the world, have stopped listening to our elders for wisdom. The oral tradition of passing family stories and lore from one generation to another is all but lost to us. And I can't help thinking that we have landed smack in the middle of a ritual void of our own.

Wising Up

I have a favorite funny story about one man's search for true Elder Wisdom.

It seems a young man journeyed all over the world, going from old sage to ancient seer, asking them all, "What is the meaning of life?" But none could answer his question. In Tibet, the Dalai Lama himself demurred but referred the seeker to a wise old hermit who lived in a cave high in the Himalayas. The young man climbed for days, through wind and rain, until he finally reached the old hermit's cave.

"Tell me, O Master," the seeker said. "What is the meaning of life?"

The old hermit scratched his beard silently for what seemed like hours before he replied.

"Life," he said finally, "is a cup of tea."

"*What?*" the young man bellowed. "I traveled around the world three times, climbed the Himalayas through wind and rain, and all you can tell me is that life is a cup of tea?"

The old hermit scratched his beard again.

"You mean it's not?" he said, shrugging.

What, in fact, could Elder Wisdom possibly consist of in today's perpetually changing, cosmopolitan world?

When I began developing the Elder Tale Program, one protest I often heard from elders was that they felt they didn't have any wisdom to convey—at least, not the kind of wisdom that anybody would take seriously. They argued that most younger people today have been exposed to more ideas through books and films, through formal education and travel, than they themselves were ever exposed to. So what could they possibly offer their children and grandchildren in the way of wisdom?

"It's a new world," one despairing grandmother said to me. "Young people today even have their own new religions. What can I tell them that they don't already know?"

Hearing her plaintive lament, I heard echoes of the Asmat elders who'd been banished from their place at the center of the circle.

There were other elders I spoke with who thought they were in possession of something that felt a bit like wisdom, but few of them trusted this feeling. Somehow most of their "wise" ideas and perceptions ended up sounding as banal as "Life is a cup of tea" when they said them out loud.

But, of course, Elder Wisdom that truly resonates cannot be summed up in pithy maxims or philosophical declarations. It does not merely consist of ideas and opinions, thought out as these may be. Elder Wisdom is, rather, the wisdom of a long life of personal experiences, a wisdom that can only be conveyed in context. And that context is stories. At first, there is the wisdom encountered in the personal insights, perceptions, and morals of a story or group of stories. But as the process goes on, as more and more stories are told and the experiences and adventures of an entire lifetime unfold, a wisdom of a deeper kind emerges—the kind that has always been called the Wisdom of Age.

Erik Erikson, the eminent psychoanalyst who has spent most of his long career studying the stages of human development, defines wisdom as a lifetime of experience well digested. In my opinion, there is no better way of going about this digestive process than gathering the stories of a lifetime and telling them to one's children and grandchildren.

I believe that the Elder Wisdom conveyed by these stories is fundamentally the same quality of wisdom that elders have passed on to new generations in every age and in every culture. It is, in some basic way, the same quality of wisdom that the Kirghiz elders pass on to their youngers in their epic songs, the same sense of continuity conveyed by !Kung elders with their tribal histories, and the same whimsical perspective and affirmation of life that transpired under the almond trees of that Spanish village I visited so many years ago. All these stories tell how a particular family or tribe came to be the way it is. They tell how a life unfolds and how a sweep of life feels. They evoke one life's mysteries and ironies, its surprises, consolations, options, and goals, its high points and low points, its conflicts and comforts. They tell, ultimately, how all of those listening fit into the life cycle. They provide maps of ways to live.

Timeless Lessons

As I worked with contemporary American families developing the Elder Tale Program, I saw timeless categories of Elder Wisdom reemerging from their newly told stories:

- The wisdom of making sense of life, of locating its meaning and appreciating its mystery.

- The wisdom of understanding the ways that a person can shape his own life and the ways in which forces outside himself shape it.

- The wisdom of personal <u>values</u>, especially those that have endured throughout an entire lifetime.

- The wisdom in grappling with and transcending life-changes: living through high points, low points, turning points, and crises.

- The wisdom of personal identity and of social connectedness: self-knowledge and social awareness.

- The wisdom of life-and-death consciousness: an inward awareness of the entire cycle of life.

- The wisdom of roots and traditions, of origins, customs, and cultural symbols.

An individual Elder Tale rarely reflects just one of these categories; typically, a story evokes elements of several kinds of wisdom. And what is "wise" about a story is not always immediately apparent. To look for wisdom in a whimsical anecdote of childhood or in a story-reconstruction of an ordinary day of sixty years ago seems like panning for gold in the kitchen sink. But wisdom is subtle stuff. It accumulates as one story links to another and then to another. And suddenly, it is there without your having to look for it.

But Who Needs It?

We all do. We are running out of wisdom. Anyone who doubts the relevance of Elder Wisdom to our society today is making a serious mistake.

As a psychoanalyst who has been deeply involved with a great many people's lives for over thirty years, I have seen how, in our society, the capacity to lead a rich, sensitive life is easily lost to an overwhelming sense of alienation and fragmentation. I have seen too many young and middle-aged people who feel cut off from the world and from their feelings; people who feel stuck on a treadmill going nowhere; people who are so riveted to short-range goals and obsessive drives that they have lost the ability to enjoy the ordinary pleasures and beauties of the world. And although these problems are psychological in one sense, I have started to think of them ultimately as problems of *dispossessed wisdom*: They are the problems of loss of philosophical perspective, problems of dislocation in time and history, problems of living in a mythological and ritual void. As Joseph Campbell's work so powerfully demonstrates, most of us today live in hunger of myths to live by. Increasingly, I believe that a significant way out of these problems and back to the world is through family stories, through a return to the rituals of Elder Wisdom.

I've seen what happens when American elders of today tell life stories to their families. It is still genuine wisdom that gets passed from one generation to the other.

Here's what one forty-two-year-old son reported to me:

"After we'd spent one Sunday afternoon with Dad, hearing his stories, I came away feeling both thrilled and disturbed. Dad had recounted some experiences he'd had during the Depression, and what really struck me was how he'd been hit so hard—had his feet knocked out from under him—but then he'd got back up and gone on the best he could. He was hit hard, but he didn't fall apart. He didn't even stop enjoying himself altogether—one wonderful story was about how he'd taken up fishing for the first time in his life to put a little food on his table and he'd had a ball doing it. . . . Well, one thing I realized listening to these stories is that I spend a lot of my life worrying that some catastrophe is going to happen and my whole world will fall apart. . . . But my own father went on, hung on, and rebuilt a life for himself. It was truly enlightening for me to look at life from that perspective for a change."

And here's what a teenage granddaughter said after several days of listening to her grandmother's stories:

"When she told us what an ordinary day was like when she was a kid, I just couldn't believe it. Her life seemed so gentle and simple and naive. . . . Well, then I started wondering: If I have kids and I tell them about my childhood back in the 1990s, will it seem as strange to them as Grandma's does to me? I mean, what's naive all depends on where you're standing at any particular time. And time keeps sailing on."

That sounded remarkably insightful to me. And that perspective, that existential sense of the relativity of time and generations, is not one that a young person is likely to gain readily in a classroom or even from a book. It is much more likely to come from hearing life stories told by a grandmother.

Another college-age granddaughter reported that her grandfather's stories—ranging from tales of an immigrant boyhood through two world wars and several careers—jolted her into appreciating what it meant to be a living link in the history of the world:

"All that stuff [Grandpa] said about his parents and their parents, going all the way back over a hundred years—well, for the first time, I really felt that I came out of all that myself. . . . Sometimes it's so easy to imagine that the world was created the day I was born and will disappear the day I die, but I can see how dangerous it is to think that way. I mean, the next step is to stop believing there are any long-range consequences to what you do in your life. And it's thinking like that that's destroyed our forests and our rivers."

Sounds like wonderfully valuable wisdom to me.

The Old Indian's Magical Dance

The wisdom of our elders, then, is still very much with us; it is simply that we as a culture have abandoned the rituals for mining it.

A significant function of ritual in a society is to give its members permission to say things that otherwise might not be said: a wedding toast, a Thanksgiving blessing, a eulogy. In some Jewish homes at the Seder dinner commemorating the emancipation of the Jews from Egypt, it is a tradition for each person at the table to take a turn saying what freedoms he is thankful for and what freedoms he still hopes for. And in most Dutch homes on Saint Nicolaas Day (he's the forerunner of our Santa Claus), family and friends write teasing, revealing poems to one another that are read out loud. Ritual communication can be the most honest, meaningful, and moving communication we have with one another. And that is why, as I was developing the Elder Tale Program, I realized that we would have to think of it as a ritual too—not only to give the Tale-Telling status and regularity, but so that important things could be said that otherwise might not be said.

But is it really possible to reinvent a ritual?

I said at the beginning of this chapter that I had been inspired by a remarkable American Indian tribe I came across in my reading. This tribe is called the Coast Salish Indians, and they live where they have always lived—in the wooded coasts and valleys of the Pacific Northwest and British Columbia. Their history is a familiar one: In premodern, "precontact" days, their elders were not only respected for their special skills—canoe-making and food processing—but for their knowledge of genealogies, family histories, myths, and rituals. In their language, the Coast Salish described someone who was successful as one "who had listened to his grandparents' stories." But then, inevitably, beginning with the first contact with Euro-American white culture, the elders quickly lost their status: Their technical knowledge was no longer relevant; their family histories and mythological knowledge was rendered instantly obsolete by imported religions.

But now here's the twist: In the last decade, all across the North American continent, Indians have been experiencing a nativist revival. Young and middle-aged Native Americans have been actively seeking their original cultural identity. And so they have turned to their elders. They want to know their own people's myths and rituals—the al-

most-lost Indian names for things, the way to make a cere-
monial mask, how to make peace with a plot of land, and
how to live a harmonious life, the kind their great-great-
grandparents lived.

Today, the Coast Salish elders are once again esteemed
by their children, grandchildren, and great-grandchildren.
They are the living repositories of tribal wisdom: the language, the stories, the rituals. One of the most important of
these rituals is the Winter Dancing Ceremony—an ancient
way of dealing with spirit possession. The elders are the
teachers and leaders of this ceremony. They stand with dignity at the center of the circle, and the others follow.

Let us follow too.

CHAPTER 2 *It's Easy to Forget How Much You Know*

————

Once when visiting Old Sturbridge Village, a living museum of nineteenth-century colonial life, I stepped into Knight's Store, where a white-haired woman in colonial garb was chatting about local goings-on as if it were a typical day in 1830. She was totally convincing, instantly transporting all of us listeners back more than a century. After she finished, she abruptly winked to a small boy in front of her who was wearing a Boston Red Sox cap.

"See the game last night?" she blurted. "Boggs couldn't hit a fly with a sledgehammer."

"Hey, that's for sure," the boy said, grinning.

On the way out, I heard the boy ask his mother, "How old was that lady?"

"Old enough to be any age she wants," his mother replied.

Smart mother. She recognized the marvelous inherent adaptability of an elder mind.

Secret Intelligence

The fact is, most elders' minds and psyches are more highly developed, freer, more flexible, expansive, creative, and philosophical than they were at any earlier stage of life. They are, in short, ideally suited to the task of telling life stories.

Yet modern medicine and psychology have been reluctant to credit the elder mind with any of these special capacities. That's because modern medicine has been too busy looking for deficits.

The prevailing medical model for a sound and bright mind is, like most everything else in our culture, based on youth. According to this model, there is little distinction between physical fitness and mental fitness: Speed and vigor prevail for both. We judge minds of all ages by the same criteria that, say, a kindergarten teacher evaluates a five-year-old's mind or an SAT exam evaluates a teenager's mind. From this standpoint, a mind is fit if it can absorb information fast and retain it for a relatively short period of time (that is, long enough to get through a test on it), and if it can make speedy calculations. Of course, these are precisely the areas where an older mind often begins to lose power as time goes on. And so elder minds are routinely dismissed as unretentive and slow—unfit and unworthy.

In fact, this evaluation is frequently self-fulfilling. If a human being of *any* age is systematically treated as mentally incompetent or uninteresting, he will soon respond accordingly. We routinely put elders in this bind: We don't expect intelligence, so they don't use it.

But what a simplistic model of an intelligent, valuable mind this is! There is no room in it for *crystallized intelligence, creative intelligence, uncensored intelligence,* or *philosophical intelligence.* And there is no room in it for wisdom.

Crystallized Intelligence

This quality of intelligence puts a premium on long-term memory rather than on short-term memory. Sure, it may now be harder for an elder to remember a telephone number, but his capacity to recall a large variety of experiences from a large variety of life periods gloriously enhances his ability to make penetrating judgments and accurate perceptions. It provides all of his thinking with depth. And depth, most of us eventually discover, is usually more valuable than speed.

Cognitive psychologist James Birren, who has pioneered studies of crystallized intelligence in elders, reports that while younger people may be quicker at performing some cognitive tasks, elders display far greater subtlety and finesse in solving problems. For example, elders fared much better in tests that required them to size up a situation and to pick out what was significant about it. Younger minds may be more facile at distinguishing the parts of things, but frequently they perceived *only* the parts. Elders proved significantly better at grasping the whole picture.

When you are searching out the themes, parallels, morals, and ironies of the experiences of a lifetime, crystallized intelligence will serve you well. As you go about developing the stories of your life, it helps enormously to be able to grasp the whole picture.

Creative Intelligence

This is the capacity to look at ideas, experiences, and problems from new angles and to make novel connections. Again, this is an aptitude that elders seem to have in abundance. While myth has it that older people are the most rigid of thinkers, that they suffer from hardening of the thought processes, recent studies show that elders tend to be more imaginative in their thinking than younger people. They seem to have a gift for what the cognitive theorists call "nonlinear" reasoning.

The source of this flexibility of mind appears to be that elders have less at stake in conforming to prevailing modes of thought. They are less intimidated by authority and less influenced by popular opinion. As Plato noted in *The Republic*, "[When we get older,] we are freed not only of one mad master, but of many." Put another way, as we get older, our thoughts, opinions, and perspectives become governed less by convention and more by choice. With the tasks of career and child-rearing finally over, with mortgages paid and deadlines met, an elder mind can roam free, unharnessed by the stresses and anxieties of earlier periods.

Unlike younger people, who often find it anxious-making to skip from one point of view to another, elders feel free to spin ideas around in their minds, taking a gander at them from every angle. The result, psychologists are now admitting, is that elders seem particularly adept at handling ambiguous situations imaginatively, at making creative connections between ideas, and at coming up with original solutions to problems. Again, these are prime talents for a storyteller.

Of course, the downside of possessing creative intelligence is that a person is apt to be accused of having a chaotic, inconsistent, and digressive mind. Elders are frequently accused of that. But one man's chaos is another man's whimsy. As the witty American philosopher Ralph Waldo Emerson once said, "A foolish consistency is the hobgoblin of little minds." And as to digressiveness, well, any artful storyteller can tell you that digression is the soul of a really good story.

Uncensored Intelligence

Similar in concept to creative intelligence, *uncensored intelligence* allows a person to see things clearly and to "call 'em the way he sees 'em." Again, the chief source of this type of intelligence is freedom from inhibitions.

"One of the best things about getting older is, I can be as eccentric as I want," one woman in her seventies told me. "And I don't mean wearing funny sneakers or feathers in my hair. I mean thinking and saying whatever I please."

Because elders feel less vulnerable to public opinion, they feel less of a need to misrepresent ideas or to alter their thoughts and perceptions in order to be acceptable.

"I'm not trying to get ahead in the world. I don't need to impress anybody," this same woman said to me with a broad smile. "I can tell the truth without consequences. What could happen? I'd lose my reputation?"

Uncensored intelligence consists not only in being able to convey the truth to others, but to oneself as well. One psychologist described its ultimate reward as "the chance of a lifetime to taste the sweetness of truth." Erik Erikson characterizes this quality of intelligence as prerequisite for self-acceptance in old age: the capacity to see oneself clearly, the bad with the good, the ordinary with the unique. Obviously, uncensored intelligence provides elders with a special genius for interpreting their lives, and for telling honest, moving stories about them.

Philosophical Intelligence

A few years back, a team of neurologists published a study asserting that the reason older people have more *philosophical intelligence* than younger people is because of the accelerated loss of their brain cells. With fewer brain cells to work with, the theory went, elders are able to attain a simpler, purer, more transcendent perspective.

I'm sure the neurologists' explanation was far more complex than that, but I still have to laugh. The only way these good doctors could admit to the fact that elders had a unique intellectual gift was by attributing it to decay. Here was just another case of modern medicine struggling vainly to reconcile its physical model of health with irrefutable mental evidence. In a way, they were just picking up where medieval witch-hunters left off.

In his seminal book *The Myth of Mental Illness*, Thomas Szasz demonstrates how society has always sought ways to put down, or better yet, *put away*, aberrant thinkers. What might have been called "sorcery" in another era, we in our era are quick to label "mental illness," or, if the person in question happens to be old, "senility." As an enlightened colleague of mine once put it, "If an older person finds it easier to recall details of his childhood than to remember what he ate for dinner last night, professionals start right away looking for signs of brain disease rather than paying close heed to a mind that is in special contact with history."

Philosophical intelligence has been described as the capacity to apprehend "the meaning of values and value of meanings." This capacity, I believe, is a natural development of living a long life and digesting it well. But it also comes from peering unflinchingly in the other direction: at death.

In his classic study *The Denial of Death,* anthropologist Ernest Becker showed how, in virtually every culture, an acute awareness of mortality increases the intensity of one's moral concerns and one's allegiance to moral beliefs. A recent survey in our own culture confirmed Becker's theory: New widows and widowers reported that their personal confrontations with death had made them more aware of life's brevity and preciousness and hence more focused on its values and meanings. Intimations of mortality deepen an elder's sense of the life cycle, of his feeling for the rhythm of change in his own life and in the generations of lives around him.

Look Back in Wonder

Along with this special aptitude for telling life stories comes an appetite for it. As we've seen, there is a culturally universal desire of elders to make contact with the generations that will survive them. This hankering to serve as a living historical link—as "generational glue"—seems, in its way, as natural as the sex drive and, ultimately, has the same goal: continuity of the species.

Telling Elder Tales satisfies a more general desire as well: the desire to remain a contributing, involved member of the society in which one lives. Like elders in the Afghanistan steppes and the Coast Salish forests, we, too, want to fulfill a societal need and be worthy of respect. We have not yet abandoned our desire for dignity.

But perhaps the most transcendent desire that impels elders to gather up their stories and give them voice is the desire to sum up. Erik Erikson identified this desire to integrate the various parts of one's life as fundamental to life's final stage. In the preceding stages, we develop our autonomy and initiative, our identity, social connections, and responsibilities. In those periods, we are busy with the business of creating ourselves and maintaining our lives, with generating careers and families and a secure place in the world. As young and middle-aged women and men, our inward thoughts tend to be psychological—analytical thoughts, schemes for reconstructing our personalities—and comparative—gauging our own lives with respect to others'. But in old age, Erikson says, we reach for a more transcendent view of ourselves, removed from self-criticism, detached from competition. Our concern, he asserts, is with "life itself, in the face of death itself."

Thus, our natural urge is to look back and review our life, to see how the sundry parts of it fit together, to make out its shape and variegated colors, to feel its sweep. We want to look back in wonder at a full life and ask, "What was my life about?" "What marks did I leave behind?" "What has made this life uniquely mine?"

It is, in short, a natural and compelling human desire to ask, "How have I been the hero of the stories of my life?"

PART II

Discovering the Hero of Your Life

"Strange, isn't it, how a man's life touches
so many other lives. When he isn't around, he
leaves an awful hole, doesn't he?"
—Clarence, the angel, in the film
It's a Wonderful Life

"There is a magic in recollection, a magic that
one feels at every age . . . in remembering we
seem to attain that impossible synthesis . . .
that life yearns for."
—Jean-Paul Sartre
Being and Nothingness, 1943

INTRODUCTION: *Core Stories*

"Whether I shall turn out to be the hero of my own life, or whether that station will be held by anybody else, these pages must show."

Whenever I read this opening passage in *David Copperfield*, I am struck both by the earnestness of the narrator's voice and by the ironic intelligence behind it. After all, who but himself could possibly be the hero of his own life?

But understanding who exactly that hero is and discovering what has made his life uniquely his own, *that* is what the pages of the novel must show. It is also, ultimately, what the best Elder Tales will tell.

The Elder Tale Program detailed in the last section of this book is constructed in such a way that you can begin telling stories to your family right now. No elaborate preparation or deep rumination is necessary to get them going. You may want to turn to that section now and read over Elder Tales I, II, and III. There is much to be said for getting started on these right away: The ice gets broken, a momentum develops, the ritual becomes established.

But beginning with Elder Tale IV, you will want to dig more deeply into yourself. You will want to immerse yourself in memory and roam about, dreaming and brooding like a poet as you search for the themes and connections that tell in profound and intimate ways who you are and what your life has been all about. This life-review process is fascinating and, for most people, it is exhilarating as well. As you begin thinking of your life as a series of interconnecting stories, your entire consciousness changes: You start making associations between experiences that you've never made before; you reexperience emotions that have lain dormant for years; you even begin to dream different kinds of dreams. And along the way, you find the stories that are uniquely your own, what I call your core stories.

Core stories are those that a novelist would choose to define you as a character. They tell the choices you made, and why, with your experiences, personality, and values, you had to make them that way. They tell the ways you changed as people and events changed around you, and they tell the ways you stayed the same in spite of them. They tell how you got what you set out to get and how you dealt with the losses and disappointments that came your way. They show your style, your quirks, your humor and passions, and how these changed from one stage of your life to the next. They dramatize how you responded to the important people in your life and how those people responded to you. They tell the ideas you believed in and the contradictions that wrestled for dominance inside your heart. They are the stories that convey the unique qualities of your life.

In the following four chapters, I offer some techniques that have proved quite valuable for seeking and identifying these core stories. Each offers a different entry-point into the world of memory and personal mythology, yet in wonderful ways all of these techniques often work together: An old photograph stimulates a new dream that makes remarkable connections between different events in your life; an old phonograph record sets off a chain of memories that leads you to a box of letters that has been sitting unopened in your attic since the Second World War. Mysterious connections, surprising discoveries—these are common occurrences as you set off in search of the hero of your life.

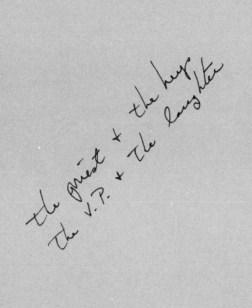

the priest + the hero
the V.P. + the laughter

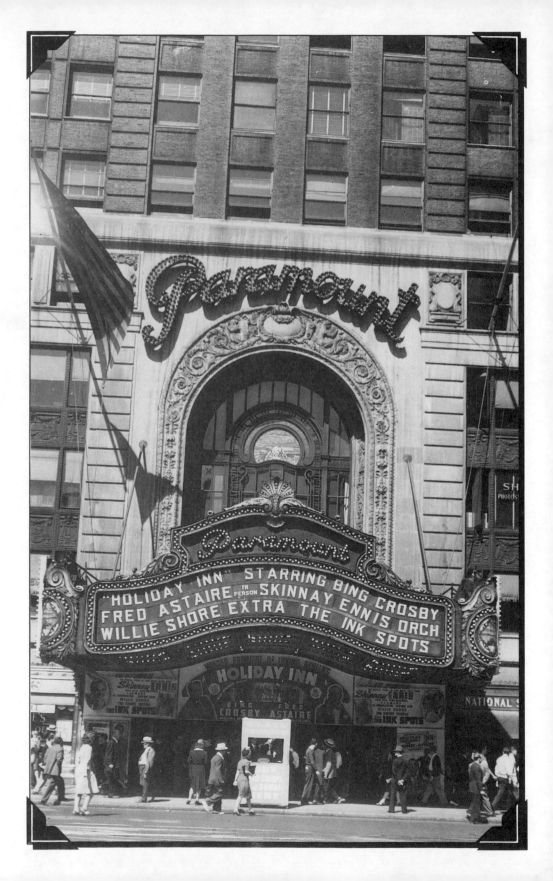

CHAPTER 3 *"Try to Remember*
That Day in September . . ."

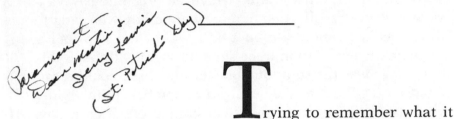

Trying to remember what it felt like to be you in, say, the autumn of 1928, or what filled your thoughts in the summer of 1936, or what your world was like in the winter of 1945, is like going on a psychic treasure hunt. Memories lie in the dunes and crevices of your mind waiting to be discovered, longing to be brought back to life.

Nothing in the mind ever completely dies, according to the ethologist Loren Eiseley. Rather, he says, disparate memories are carried "back and forth in the desert of a billion neurons, set down, picked up and dropped again. . . . You will only find the bits and cry out because they were yourself."

But there are maps to help you find your way in that neuron desert, signposts to help you locate those lost bits of yourself: mnemonic prompters, souvenirs, guided-memory techniques. In the course of developing the Elder Tale Program, certain of these prompters and techniques proved particularly useful, some that we expected, others that surprised us.

Private Words

"Dear Diary," a friend of mine named Irene wrote in a linen-covered notebook some fifty-five years ago. "I just want you to know that I will love Lester Borden with all my heart for the rest of my life."

Reading this entry at the age of sixty-eight, Irene broke into uproarious laughter. She couldn't for the life of her remember who Lester Borden was. So much for eternal love.

But then she read on. There Lester was again in the next entry and in the next. In fact, Lester appeared for an entire month of entries, after which he precipitously vanished. A vague recollection of a red-haired boy who sang to himself as he bounced a rubber ball against the steps of his porch finally emerged in Irene's memory. And although this lone image was the sum total of everything she could recall about Lester Borden, she began to remember quite vividly what it felt like to have an all-consuming crush on a boy. She remembered the breathlessness of it, the constant chatter with her friends about it, the thrill of having something outside her own family that mattered so much. Prodded by her diary, Irene was remembering what it felt like to be herself at the age of thirteen.

Diaries, journals, marginal notes to yourself in favorite books—all such confidential messages to yourself are, of course, prime sources of memories and the stories that go with them. In fact, many of these messages were committed to paper with at least some consciousness of addressing a future self. "Remember me as I am now!" they seem to say. "Don't betray me with some 'mature' reconstruction of who you think I was or should have been."

One old friend I know actually came across an entry he wrote in his journal at the age of seventeen that began, "I'll probably read this when I'm fat and bald and smirk at it like Father smirks at me now. But both of you be damned!"

What a remarkably insightful seventeen-year-old this man had been. The fact is, we often do have trouble bringing ourselves to look at old diaries precisely because we are embarrassed by our youthful selves. "Oh God, I was so young, so naive, so self-involved, so silly!" we think, and close the diary without letting our young selves speak further to us.

But what if we do seem silly and naive to ourselves now? That is not how we felt to ourselves then.

Try to remember what it felt like to set down in your diary the thoughts that you did: What notions circulated in your mind? What seemed ridiculous, and what made you furious? What did the world look like through your eyes? Be charitable with your young self, and try to remember.

And prepare to be surprised by what you do remember. Irene could barely recall her erstwhile eternal flame, Lester, but she could remember her overwhelming feelings of teenage infatuation, which, in turn, led to several stories, including a fine one about hiding in the choir loft during a baptism and whispering about boys with her friend the pastor's daughter. Often, the best story that comes back to you in this exercise is not the one that you wrote down in your diary, but one that you were led to by a chain of associations that began with a diary entry.

Don't stop with diaries. Clues to your younger self can be found in what appear to be the most insignificant notations to yourself.

"I confess to feeling an odd little private thrill when I found a ragged notebook that included Roger Casement's laundry list for the 12th of May in 1899 in Loanda on the west coast of Africa," writes the biographer B. L. Reid. "I felt my nostrils flaring: I had been granted a quick intimation that seemed to be olfactory, a whiff of the real dailiness of a British consul's life in tropical parts and Victorian times."

Real dailiness. That's the stuff that the most evocative Elder Tales are made of: what you ate for breakfast, what your family did together after dinner, what your house smelled like on laundry day. For Elder Tale III of the program ("A Day in Your Life"), in particular, memories of real dailiness are critical, so you might want to search through old notebooks and paper scraps for your own old laundry lists, shopping lists, daily agendas, and school notes. Incidentally, if people have saved nothing else they've written, most have managed to hold on to some of their old school reports and drawings. Give these a good lookover too. There may be clues here to the way you thought about the world back then, as well as to memories of teachers and classmates. And, as is true for any item you have recorded in your own hand, the mere sight of your young handwriting may excite your memory.

We tend to save old letters too—save them, but never read them. Old correspondence from family, friends, and lovers are obviously mines of memories, but again, many of us find that we are reluctant to open up those dusty boxes in the attic and reread a letter of thirty, forty, or fifty years ago. We are afraid, I think, of the feelings that the letters may elicit. The writer of that love letter may be long lost or dead. Your relationship with the author of that whole stack of letters may have ended badly. There is, of course, always a bittersweetness in any reminder that we once were young and never shall be again, and letters, for some reason, can be more disturbing than other reminders in this regard.

Yet I say, Open up those boxes and read those letters. No one I've ever known who went back and reread his old correspondence has regretted it. Strong feelings arise, yes, but the abiding feelings are almost always of a sublime connectedness to the people of your past. *Letters are documented intimacy*. That people write them so infrequently today will be an inestimable loss later when they seek to reconstruct the stories of their own lives. And, oh, the stories you will find folded inside those envelopes, stories about the most important people in your life and your relationship to them, stories that you really couldn't think of abandoning on that neuron desert.

Another place to look is in an old address book—the older the better. I guarantee a deluge of memories as you scan the names, some going back thirty or more years. Recently, as I was addressing my Christmas cards, it happened to me. There was the name "Charlie Wilder" in my address book—my old college roommate—and suddenly I was remembering us singing together in the glee club, giving a concert at Town Hall in New York; then I remembered that we sang that entire concert again, impromptu, right in Grand Central Station at two in the morning. What a sound! I'd almost forgotten that wonderful night.

Lying somewhere between private words and public objects are high school and college yearbooks, replete with jokes and reminiscences from the hands of your old classmates; old newspaper clippings, yellowed and flaking, documenting achievements and honors (and perhaps a few dishonors) of yourself or family members; and scrapbooks that you or your parents put together of trips and events that someone back then knew should be recorded for posterity. These are all, of course, rich sources for Elder Tales.

Don't Forget the Souvenirs

It's a rectangular piece of cloth, less than a yard long, threadbare, and so faded you can barely make out the chicken-scratch lines and crosses printed on one side of it.

"It looks like a worn-out rag. No wonder somebody is always trying to throw it out on me," an elder named Frank told me, smiling.

But that rag is a scarf that was issued to Frank and to all his fellow paratroopers in Operation Market Garden, the Allies' daring 1944 attempt to get behind the German defense lines in North Holland and secure the bridges on the Waal River. Because paper maps of the roads and bridges would have gotten wet and torn, the army printed the maps for Market Garden on these scarves, which the men tied around their necks before vaulting out of their airplanes. It is not a piece of cloth that Frank would ever think of throwing away.

"Of course, there's no way I'd forget Market Garden even if I didn't have [the scarf]," he says. "But sometimes I can hold it in my hand and something new will come back to me—something I saw, maybe some words that one of my buddies said before the shooting started. There's something about touching it, you know, that does that."

The word *souvenir* has become so associated with the trinkets sold in tourist shops that we sometimes forget that it means "to remember" in French, literally to "come back" to mind. A genuine souvenir, like Frank's scarf, does just that—it brings a time and place back to mind. And often it works through the senses in a way that a photograph or the written word cannot.

The writer Toni Morrison speaks of our "emotional memory. What the nerves and skin remember . . ." Objects from our past are a tap-line into that emotional memory.

A prep-school friend of mine recently tried on a baseball glove that he used to put on almost daily some forty-five years ago. He punched the old glove with his fist, smacked a baseball into it a few times, slapped it against his knee, put it to his nose, and inhaled deeply, catching an aroma across time of sweat-soaked leather. And he was flooded with memories: teammates he hadn't thought of in as many years, a cheer the girls used to call out, even a particular game in which he'd made a crucial play. His nerves, skin, ears, and nose were all remembering.

Speaking of noses, it has been said of the American memoirist Alfred Kazin, that he "wrote with his nose." He could convey, for example, "how his father's overalls smelled of shellac and turpentine when he came home from his job as a housepainter." Such sensory details are what make a time and place come alive for a story listener; they make it real.

Virtually every object you've retained over the years, whether on purpose or not, has a story attached to it: a matchbook, a menu, a program, a ticket stub, a receipt, a dance card, a floorplan, a recipe, a trophy, an icon, a baptismal gown, a wooden top, a silver spoon, a candy wrapper, a sketch, a sampler. The things you find packed away in those boxes piled in your attic, between the pages of your old books, in the back of your pantry drawers, or inside your old steamer trunk—all of these carry stories with them.

You can find souvenirs in some of the newer "antique" shops too. (I can't quite get myself to take the quotation marks off that word when it refers to shops that stock items that were brand-new when I was a child.) These days such shops seem to carry more "everyday" and popular items, like commercial oatmeal tins, children's toys and games, gasoline-station calendars, and roadside signs. In one, I saw a series of five such signs, which read, respectively, "Every day," "we do our part," "to make your face," "a work of art," concluding with the inevitable "Burma Shave." Just about everyone who took car trips with his parents on American highways in the thirties and forties has some "Burma Shave" memories and some stories about family vacations to go with them.

Take your time with souvenirs. A familiar activity involving an object from the past can activate what is called kinesthetic memory—the memory that resides in muscle movement. A man I know named Steve, whose entire life has revolved around horses, finds himself involuntarily remembering scenes from his past when he takes out a very old harness and puts it on a horse or when he greases the wheels of his old hay wagon. His body remembers.

So don't simply turn your old silver pocket watch over in your hand—wind it up, put it to your ear, slip it in your pocket, and pull it out again. Or set up that old box camera your father brought with him from Czechoslovakia. There is no film for it, to be sure, but go through a pantomime as if there were, eye to the viewer, hand on the shutter lever. Memories will follow.

Undress and dress that wooden doll. Make some tea in that samovar your mother brought with her from Russia. Fit a candle into that silver candlestick holder that was given to you as a wedding gift, now light it. See if you can still get into those lace-up shoes. Throw that black silk cape across your shoulders. Pack that old suitcase. Grip your old passport tightly in your hand as if you were once again a young teenager just off the boat from Poland passing through Ellis Island. Memories will follow.

In Elder Tale III, "A Day in Your Life," I suggest that some elders might want to tell stories to their families *while* performing some activity from their past, say, baking a strudel or making ice cream by hand. The activity not only serves as a demonstration to listeners, but it brings back to mind story details and, sometimes, whole stories to the teller.

Media Memories

An elder I know named Margot was leafing through a picture book titled *This Fabulous Century* when she suddenly stopped and laughed out loud. A bit embarrassing, considering she was in the public library, but Margot couldn't help herself. She had just turned the page to a photo of a young flapper wearing a rain slicker with a young man kneeling behind her painting a picture on it.

"Slicker painting! That was all the rage when I was a young woman," Margot told me. "Good Lord, I hadn't thought about that in a million years. What a hoot!"

But now that she did think of it, hoot and all, Margot remembered quite a bit more: who had painted her own slicker, what had become of him, the winter she had ended up wearing that same slicker over sweaters because she'd had to sell her raccoon coat to help pay her tuition at teachers' college—a chain of personal associations prompted by a photograph of a perfect stranger, associations that produced some marvelous stories.

The shelves of your local library are loaded with memory-joggers, period photo books being an excellent place to start. There are classics like Walker Evans's stark documentation of the Depression, *Let Us Now Praise Famous Men*. And then there are classics of a different sort, those compilations of photographs and captions culled from old issues of magazines that have come and gone (and, in many cases, come again) like *Life, Look, Saturday Evening Post, Vanity Fair, Liberty*, and *Collier's*. Such magazines help recall the texture of times past, the structure, details, and trivia of the daily world you lived in: the clothes you wore, the songs you listened to, the dances you danced, the advertisements for products that once resided inside your icebox and medicine chest, the sport teams you rooted for, the celebrities whose romances you followed in the papers, and, a personal favorite of mine, the crazes of the day—the flagpole sittings and dance marathons. Any of these can lead you directly to personal recollections, to your own stories in the context of those times.

Another kind of compilation that gets my memory going is a book of old cartoons, like *The New Yorker* albums. A Morgan drawing of a speakeasy, a Birnbaum caricature of Olsen and Johnson, Thurber's "The War Between Men and Women" series—these not only remind me of the events and people of the period, but of contemporary attitudes toward them. And, of course, they lead me to personal stories. Looking at an old Peter Arno cartoon that twitted the attitude of the rich toward Franklin Roosevelt, I suddenly remembered a well-to-do boarding school friend of mine who used to make disparaging jokes about FDR, but who I discovered crying in his room on the day that President Roosevelt died. It was, I believe, one of the first times in my young life that I appreciated how very contradictory people's feelings could be.

Most libraries can also supply you with microfilmed copies of old issues of newspapers and magazines. If, for "A Day in Your Life," you have selected a specific date, say, May 12, 1932, the day of your sixteenth birthday, it can be both helpful and fascinating to read the newspaper of that day. What were the front-page headlines, and what did they mean to you? What did it cost to buy a dress? What books were popular? What movies were playing? You are apt to find clues to memories in surprising places too—in the classified ads, the "Miss Lonelyhearts" column, the obituaries.

There are now mail-order archival services that can supply you with an actual copy of a newspaper from a specific date. It's a bit expensive, but there is nothing quite like sitting down in your easy chair with, say, *The New York Times* of fifty years ago, and turning the pages one at a time, casually reading "the news of the day." How easy it is to slip through the time warp, to feel that no time has passed at all. Your consciousness changes, even your body feels a bit different, and memories can come back vividly, full of feeling and nuance, remembered as if they happened just yesterday.

Another memory-jogger available at your library is the novels that you read at earlier stages of your life. Perhaps leafing through the book reviews of old newspapers has reminded you of your favorites of times past, say *Mayfair* or *Forever Amber* or *The Young Lions*. Finding an old book that once meant a great deal to you and rereading it now can evoke a variety of dormant memories and feelings. Many elders have reported to me that this is a powerful tool for revisiting their minds of an earlier stage of life; rereading a book can slip them back to the mind and eye with which they originally read it.

"I vaguely remembered that *Of Human Bondage* had made quite an impression on me when I was a young man," an elder named Gilbert reported to me. "But picking it up and reading it now, I could actually remember how certain passages had struck me back then. Some of those passages had been thunderbolts for me—like one where the hero, Philip Carey, finally sorts out the difference between love and passion. I realize now that some of the ideas I read in that book stayed with me, sort of crystallized a few thoughts of my own, and probably influenced a couple of important choices in my own life—maybe even who I married."

Later, when Gilbert was preparing Elder Tale VI of the program, "Epiphanies and Lessons," his rereading of *Of Human Bondage* provided him with several valuable insights into the development of his own ideas and the personal choices that followed from them.

There are, of course, books being written all the time that evoke periods of the past. These, too, can set off a chain of personal associations that bring back the stories of your own life. Reading, say, E. L. Doctorow's detail-filled novel *World's Fair* can drop the reader right onto the streets and into the kitchens and parlors of the New York City of 1939. The author provides the landscape where a reader with a similar background can let his memory roam; the author's landmarks point the way to your own personal stories.

By the way, be sure to bring a notebook and pen with you on your library visits. Memories can explode in your mind without warning; get your key story points down on paper before they fade away.

Packaged Nostalgia

In recent years, packaged nostalgia has begun to appear on the shelves of gift and record shops in the form of audiotapes of old radio broadcasts. (That much bandied-about word *nostalgia* has made me smile ever since Simone Signoret titled her memoirs *Nostalgia Isn't What It Used to Be*.) The package sometimes includes a tape player disguised as on old cathedral radio on which you can play the old shows; it's contrived, but it can be wonderfully effective. Sit back, "tune in" to an old Edgar Bergen and Charlie McCarthy show, and marvel at that innocent suspension of disbelief that once allowed you and most everyone else across America to be entertained by a ventriloquist *on radio*. Close your eyes and laugh your way through the Jack Benny or Fred Allen show, complete with "live" commercials; listen again to that World Series game that once seemed the most important event of your life; or sing along with an entire *Your Hit Parade* ending with Sinatra's reprise of "Put Your Dreams Away for Another Day." Put on Orson Welles's infamous radio hoax, *Invasion from Mars,* and remember the terror that crept through your own living room when your family first heard it. Or listen again to President Truman's announcement of the bombing of Hiroshima and recall how you and your family responded to that news. Specific memories of what you were doing and thinking when you listened to these broadcasts for the first time may come back to you, but perhaps even more important, listening to these broadcasts now can help you become what I call "willfully disoriented"—a key to the memory-recall technique of time-rambling that I discuss later on.

The video-rental shop is a relatively new and, I find, terrifically exciting source of media memories. You can pick out a favorite movie from the past and view it again, tapping into the eyes, thoughts, and sensibilities of the younger "you" who first saw it.

"The other day I saw *Adam's Rib* again for the first time in what must be forty years," an elder named Iris told me. "Good Lord, that's a funny movie, and about as up-to-date about the war between the sexes as anything. . . . I remember [my husband] and I had one doozy of a fight after we saw that movie together in town. Carried on for hours, just like Tracy and Hepburn. . . ."

The movie reminded Iris about how frequently she and her late husband used to fight about movies, newspaper stories, and the like, and how much she secretly enjoyed those fights. Later, when she was telling tales of her marriage to her family, she was able to reconstruct some of those "Tracy and Hepburn" fights that she and her husband used to have.

"Sometimes I think couples had better fights then," she told her children and grandchildren. "More wit and less meanness. We were always fighting back our smiles as much as we were fighting each other."

Like period novels, films that re-create the past can evoke personal memories too. *Field of Dreams* did that for some friends of mine who grew up in the Midwest in the twenties; *Enemies: A Love Story* did it for friends who lived through the forties in Brooklyn. And an early Technicolor musical about an even earlier time, *Meet Me in St. Louis*, evokes multigenerational American family life for those whose memories go back to near the beginning of the century. There are hundreds of period movies; you might want to get one of the catalogs that describe those that are on videotape and choose which are most likely to speak to your own experiences. In Chapter 5, I'll discuss how movies and books can go beyond merely stimulating memories—how some can inform and shape the very process of life review itself.

Old newsreels are also available in most video-rental shops, including the dramatic *March of Time* series. I remember seeing one of those on the subject of torture machines that gave me nightmares for an entire week; that, of course, didn't prevent me from returning to the theater the following Saturday for the next installment. In addition, there are many documentaries assembled out of old footage, like *Victory at Sea*, that can awaken memories in the same way that period photography books do.

Public Spaces, Private Memories

Recently, a colleague told me about an experiment in which a neurolinguistic programmer had placed a group of elders in a painstakingly constructed environment where everything was twenty-five years out of date. Inside this multiroom space, it was 1966: The furnishings, the products, the food in the fridge, the programs on the radio, the magazines on the coffee table—everything dated from 1966, and everything was new.

On the first day of living there, most of the elders were excited, but also somewhat disoriented. By the end of the second day, most had begun to reestablish some familiar daily routines of twenty-five years ago. And by the end of the fourth day, *every one of them claimed to feel significantly younger than he or she had felt in years.*

Many could actually perform physical tasks that had been too difficult for them only a week before. And virtually all of them could remember details of their personal life of twenty-five years ago as if they had happened only yesterday.

The implications of this experiment boggle the mind. At first blush, the setup seems like a quick fix for many of the ills of old age. Yet on second look, some creepy, science-fictiony aspects of the experiment come into focus; in order for this artificial environment to have maximum effect, everything and everyone from the "present" world have to be excluded. Still, I cannot help but be intrigued by the experiment's suggestion that some residual part of our younger self remains inside us no matter how old we get. I like that idea. It's as if whatever triggers our memory can trigger the responses and physical capacities of this younger self inside us too.

In the last few years, some new museums have re-created "total environments" that work on all our senses, pulling us back to points in the past. Arriving by ferry at the new Ellis Island Immigration Museum, visitors enter a restored baggage room piled high with vintage trunks, suitcases, and baskets, and from there move directly into the Registry Room, a large hall empty save for some benches and the inspector's desk, the original furnishings. This room looks and feels and echoes sounds just the way it did at the beginning of the century. It is the emotional core of the museum. It is here where immigrants returning to Ellis Island find themselves suddenly slipping back through time, bombarded with memories, awash with feelings.

"Suddenly, my heart was pounding inside me, just like it had sixty years ago," a woman named Isabella reported. "I remembered it all—sitting on that bench, waiting hours for my mother to come for me. She had been in America for six years already. I couldn't remember what she looked like. Finally, this very pretty woman in a white hat came up to me and said, 'Hello, Isabella. You can come home now.' . . . I told this story to my grandchildren right in that very same room. The youngest one, she started to cry."

It is little wonder that from the day that Ellis Island reopened for visitors, it was a place where entire families came to hear their elders' tales. This is literally what the museum was made for.

In Elder Tale IX, "Sentimental Journeys," I outline a plan wherein elders return to important landmarks of their past, both to tap directly into memories and to tell their stories in the context of where they happened. Incidentally, I've noticed that these journeys often have an interesting side effect: They make people feel younger.

Time Rambling

You are sitting back in your favorite easy chair browsing through a copy of *The New York Times* from forty years ago. On your tape recorder, *Your Hit Parade* from approximately the same date is playing a hit of the day. You sing along, then sigh, let your eyes flutter closed, and sigh again. . . .

All the kids were still at home then. Billy would be taking advantage of the late summer sun and still be shooting baskets out in the driveway. Patty would be listening to the show with you, sitting on the rug, tapping her hand against her shoe tops. . . . What would she be wearing? What would Kate be making for dinner? . . . You can almost smell it. . . .

If the above sounds like a setup for self-hypnosis, you are not far from the mark. It is a description of "time rambling," a memory-stimulating technique that promotes a kind of altered state of consciousness somewhere between a dream and a reverie. The goal is to become "willfully disoriented," to lose yourself in a different period of your life. You are trying to slip into a daydream where the past feels as though it is the present, yet to consciously guide that daydream, to aim your inner eye like a movie camera at places where you think stories might be lurking. In fact, when it works well, time rambling feels a bit like watching a movie of your past. . . .

There's a car rumbling to a stop in front of the house. It's Digby, Kate's brother. . . . Five years since he came home from the war, and he still doesn't seem to have his feet on the ground. Always dropping by to shoot baskets with Billy and then waiting for Kate to ask him to join us for dinner. God, Kate worries about him. Thinks he'll never amount to anything, and he was so capable, too, she says. Just last week she asked me what I thought about having him move in with us. I said, Okay, but I didn't like the idea. . . . Oh yes, it was an evening just like this one—Digby comes in with Billy for dinner and announces that he got this letter from his old navy friend in California who is buying his own vineyard. He wants Digby to come out there and work with him. . . . Seven years later, Digby was a wealthy man, married with a family of his own. . . . Sometimes I'd say to Kate, just to kid her, maybe we ought to go out there and move in with Digby. . . .

Stories like this one, stories that reveal the cares, ironies, and drama of your family's life, surface as you ramble about in your past, freely associating from a song to a lived-in atmosphere to the story-worthy events of your life.

It is not necessary to use such mnemonic devices as an old newspaper or radio show to start you rambling. Many friends of mine can do it by simply finding a quiet, comfortable spot, closing their eyes, and gently calling up a particular period of their life detail by detail—say, the pictures on the wall, the sounds in the street, a familiar voice.

Try it. Imagine a particular scene from your life and then run it and rerun it in your mind like a movie, over and over, tuning in all your senses, gathering in details until it feels as if you are actually in that time and place again. For example, try as best you can to put yourself back in your grade school, then in a particular classroom, then in the desk and chair where you sat. Can you see it? See who is sitting beside you? This technique has proved particularly helpful for Elder Tale VIII, "Telegrams and Epitaphs," wherein you search for the stories of the "minor characters" of your life. Incidentally, as always, have a notebook or memo-recorder on hand to note down the stories that come back to you afterward.

There are some people who find the idea of time rambling a bit scary. They are afraid of losing control, as if they would be hallucinating on a mind-altering drug. Some have expressed a fear of "getting stuck" in the past like a character in *Back To The Future*. In response, all I can say is that no time rambler I have known has ever had such problems; everyone comes back, often feeling refreshed. Still, if you have lingering fears, you might want to have someone nearby when you try this technique the first time, someone to anchor you in the present, or you might want to set an alarm clock to go off after a half hour or so, to "snap" you back to the present. Once reassured that you don't really lose control at all, you'll probably feel easier—and more adventurous—the next time you go time rambling for the stories of your life.

Programmed Questions and Collective Remembering

I've come across a number of handbooks for prodding the memory that offer page after page of specific questions to consider, like, "When you ran away from home, where did you go?" and "How did you learn to whistle?" and "Who was your most revolting relative?"

And there is at least one software program I am aware of that asks the diligent memoirist to record his answers to several hundred questions in his computer. "Begin . . . by typing the phrase: 'I was born on . . . ' and then complete the sentence with the day and date of your birth" the initial message on the screen says.

Both the books and the software have their value; they

certainly can lead you down memory tracks you may have missed. But I should also warn you of what I consider the severe limitations of this Q&A approach to locating memories. On its own, it promotes a linear, nonassociative way of thinking; once a question is answered, the tendency is to go on immediately to the next one rather than to see what linking thoughts and memories come to mind. You are apt to start thinking of your life in terms of a list, and although this list might be cute and entertaining in spots, a list is nothing at all like a story. It hasn't the shape or feeling of one, and ultimately it has no genuine authorship. In fact, it is not even really your own list; it is simply your responses to the questioner's list.

My worst objection is to the idea of producing your life story by filling in blanks *alone in a room with a computer.* That image is the very antithesis of what the Elder Tale Program is all about. Obviously, we'll all be spending a good deal of time alone as we roam through our memories and prepare our stories. But our fundamental goal is to tell these stories out loud to our families, to personally pass them along, not to solitarily file them away on a magnetic disk.

Perhaps the best use I've found for memory question lists is to generate planned "reminiscence conversations." Such conversations can be a fabulous source of stories if you have a family member or friend with whom you've shared experiences who is currently available to you. I first heard about reminiscence conversations as a preplanned technique from a friend named Karl who had found he was placing several phone calls a day to his sister while he was putting together the Elder Tales of his childhood.

"I'd call her up to ask if she could remember the name of my first-grade teacher, and along with the answer she'd remember some story about [the teacher], and that would remind me of something else. This could go on for quite a while. I'd remember things I could never seem to think of on my own. Then, a couple of hours later, I'd call her again to see if she could remember whatever happened to our old dog, Daisy, and we'd start trading stories again."

Finally, my friend suggested to his sister that they dedicate an afternoon just to digging up stories from their common past, and, when they did, they discovered that the best way to keep the stories coming was to have questions to prod them along. So, whenever they ran out of their own questions, they'd turn to one of the memory-jogging books and read out, say "What bedtime stories do you remember Mother telling us?" or "Which tablecloth did she save for special occasions?," and that would get their stories going again.

More recently, I've heard of clubs, some of them veterans' organizations, that organize evenings of reminiscence conversations. Like Karl, many of the participants say that these evenings allow them to remember things they felt they never could have remembered on their own. They seem to have a wonderful time at it too. Still, as I chastened Karl, be sure not to leave your stories there—your children and grandchildren are waiting to hear them.

Chapter 4 *Photoanalysis*

———

Photographs are mirrors with memories. They reflect ourselves back to ourselves across time. They show us where we were, who we were with, and what we were like at various stages of our life. And taken in a chronological series of different points in a lifetime, they show how we—and our relationships—have changed and evolved over the years.

I knew from the start that photos would play a major role in the gathering and telling of modern-day Elder Tales. Clearly, photographs are the memory-joggers par excellence. We pull an old snapshot we haven't looked at in fifty years out of a dusty shoebox, and suddenly a long-forgotten moment flashes in our memory.

I was six-
teen at the
time, and we
were all work-
ing in the Gai-
ter Factory,
making gaiters,
little short
things they used
to wear, leg
coverings. We
got paid very
little, I don't
remember how
much. It was so
little I guess I
don't even re-

member. . . . This was a pretty happy time, a picnic in the park. That is Eva Merril next to me. She was my best friend. . . . Of course, she's passed away now.

Here I am seventy years later, celebrating my birthday . . . surrounded by my great-grandchildren. Life has been good to me. The good Lord can take me when he wants—I'm ready, but it's just wonderful I'm still living.

Out of such photographs, long and fascinating stories begin. The memories encapsulated within the borders of a single snapshot can set in motion dozens upon dozens of stories.

Stop-Time

While there is much in the past century of our society's history that has turned us away from fully appreciating the richness of personal memories, nothing in the history of mankind—save the creation of written language—can compare with the invention of the camera as a tool for evoking and compiling personal memories. In the pre-camera era, very few people possessed concrete images of themselves, their friends, or their family as they existed in prior stages of life. Unless one was an artist or a rich man, he was unlikely to own a drawing, painting, or sculpture of himself as a youngster or as a young adult. His only access to an image of his face as it appeared decades earlier was his memory of looking at himself in a mirror—an incredibly difficult image to retain over a lifetime of looking in mirrors.

As we've seen, we have many other tools to jog our memories, but for sheer *volume*, for sheer *coverage* of all the stages of one's life, and for sheer *availability*, none of these tools can compare with photographs. I haven't yet encountered a family that does not have at least a handful of old photographs stashed away in a box, envelope, or album somewhere. And most families, I've found, are in possession of whole drawersful—even desksful—of them, most of which they have not looked at in years.

One of the main reasons people haven't looked at their boxes of old photographs, they tell me, is because it makes them feel guilty that they haven't *done* anything with them. This usually means that they haven't labeled them and stuck them in albums as they've been intending to do "someday" over the past forty or so years. Well, as you embark on the Elder Tale adventure, you can dispense with that particular guilt. This program provides you with plenty to do with all those old photographs, yet it doesn't require any of the tedium of cataloguing and pasting them if that's not what you feel like doing.

In Elder Tales I and II of the program—"Snapshots from Your Youth" and "Snapshots from Your Adult Years"—we'll use photographs primarily for their mnemonic value: to summon up memories and the stories immediately attached to them, to call up the atmosphere of a time and the feel of a place, to remind us of people who had almost slipped away completely into the forest of forgotten faces.

One of my fondest memories was watching Mammy sit before her mirror, brushing her long, long hair, and then braiding it before going to bed. . . . I loved her so much.

and

Oh God, there's Charlie, under the table. Typical—lapping up the family secrets. If that dog could talk . . .

Photograph in hand, time stops, memories begin.
But that is *just* a beginning.

Frozen Moments, Hidden Stories

Over twenty years ago, I developed a method of analyzing photographs for hidden psychological meanings that I called *photoanalysis*. I had found that photographs, like dreams, slips of the tongue, body language, and handwriting, can reveal remarkable hidden aspects of a personality and of relationships. As images frozen in time, they offer us a unique opportunity to methodically and deeply study them. Like detectives, we can analyze a photograph for clues to secret affections and inner conflicts, anxieties and aspirations, as well as for the psychological seeds of personal developments that were still to come at the time that the photograph was taken.

For starters, the human face is capable of displaying thousands of different expressions, each of which has something to say about us, about how we react to the world around us. Further, we now know that body language speaks loudly, that voluntary as well as involuntary expressions in movement, posture, and muscle tension can accurately reflect the inner feelings and motivations of people. Words can lie, but—with extremely rare exceptions—the body does not.

Photography can capture every one of those expressions and physical attitudes, whether we intend it to do so or not. But even more important, a photo offers a pure visual experience that is not contaminated, distorted, or distracted by words or movement. You can go over a photograph time and time again, and every time you look at it, you can discover new meanings, new experiences, new sensations—if you know how. But most of us don't really look—we are visually illiterate.

In its original conception, the primary goals of photoanalysis fell into four general categories:

To determine the reality of past experiences and help correct distortions of memory

By this, I don't simply mean the corroboration or disputation of straight facts, such as how old one was when the family vacationed at Niagara Falls or who exactly came to your First Communion. Rather, I see a close examination of photographs as a way to test the assumptions of old myths and what I call "the family version" of the way things were.

For example, a patient of mine named Mark used to speak frequently of having been a withdrawn and frightened child.

"My mother always said that I was the shy one and [my brother] was the outgoing, happy one," he told me.

One day on a hunch, I asked Mark to bring in as many photographs of himself up to the age of ten that he could put his hands on. He came in the next time with a bellows-folder loaded with snapshots. We spread them out on the couch and began going over them, one by one.

Among the very first photos I looked at was one that showed Mark at the age of six or seven in full cowboy regalia pointing a play pistol at a distant target.

"If you could choose one word to characterize the boy in this picture, what would it be?" I asked.

Mark shrugged. "*Defensive?*" he suggested.

"Looks more like *aggressive* or *defiant* to me. And certainly not *shy* or *frightened*," I said.

"But after all, I *was* posing," Mark countered.

"Look at the determination in that gaze, the defiance in those eyes. Look at the confidence in the stance of those legs and in the direct bead that boy is taking with his gun. If that's merely acting, I'll eat a cowboy hat," I said.

In a variety of ways, several more photographs of young Mark challenged the "family version" of him as a withdrawn and frightened child. Perhaps he had been quite shy at times, but spread out before us was documented evidence of a boy who also could be defiant, willful, silly, and boisterous. Photoanalysis made that abundantly clear. As I

expected would happen, Mark found this exercise wonderfully emotionally liberating. It also liberated dozens of near forgotten stories about this "other" Mark, the Mark who didn't conform to the family myth of himself that he had accepted uncritically for so many years.

Photoanalysis has proved remarkably effective at providing a fresh perspective on the past for a great many people I've worked with. A forgotten photograph of a mother warmly pressing a little girl to her breast literally astounded that now-thirty-year-old daughter who could only remember rejection and coldness from her mother. A photograph of a festive birthday party in a Quonset hut supplied a sixty-one-year-old man with more clear signs of both the poverty he grew up in and the brave joy his parents created within those curved metal walls than he had ever remembered before.

Correcting a recollection of the past makes it richer, the memory more complex. In a single photograph, one can see how apparent contradictions like love and rejection or poverty and joy can coexist.

To pinpoint times of significant change in behavior, feelings, attitude, and physical appearance

One rarely changes in a mirror. You may look at yourself once a day every day for eighty years and not once say with certainty, Ah, I look older than yesterday, or wiser or more mature. Most of the changes in our life come by infinitesimal degrees: millimeters of physical growth, milligrams of personality alteration. And yet by studying our photographs, we can detect and isolate many of the significant turning points of our lives.

One way we can try to locate these turning points is by comparing photographs of ourselves at different times in our life and looking for changes that occurred in the intervals between them. The most obvious changes, of course, are physical. Seeing yourself robust-looking one year, drawn and thin the next, you can isolate a period of ill health or, perhaps, deprivation in your life. And, to be sure, you will see changes in style—the clothes you wore and how you wore them. In itself, this can be a clue to other changes in your life, like your financial and professional status.

But studied carefully, a chronological series of photographs can reveal subtler transformations: changes in attitudes and character—even changes in values. Read acutely, time-lapsed differences in body language and expression can point to changes in such traits as confidence, shame, hopefulness, and despair. And certainly a series of group photographs offers clues to changes in interpersonal relationships—change, say, in affection and estrangement or trust and wariness between people.

Seeing that a significant change has occurred during an interval of time, we inevitably ask ourselves, What happened between this picture and that one that accounts for this change? Often, with the aid of the photographs, this question shakes loose near-forgotten episodes in our lives, changes of circumstance and relationships, or perhaps personal realizations and resolutions that marked the beginning of a new trajectory in our lives.

The other main way that photoanalysis can pinpoint critical junctures in our lives is by helping us recollect the emotional impact of a particular moment that is recorded in a *single* photograph. I've found that a surprising number of people instinctively record the important transitional moments of their lives on film. Obviously, this is true of traditional rites of change, like graduation or wedding day. But there are other, subtler transitional moments we record, the significance of which we can only appreciate in retrospect.

This is a photograph of Ann, my wife of forty years, taken the summer we fell in love with each other. There she is, standing in front of her cabin at the riding camp where I was an instructor. She is poised and demure, but with an undeniable expression of eagerness and expectation on her lovely face. Looking at that picture now, she can recall how she felt at the time: excited and proud. She remembers knowing then that her life would never be the same after that summer; she tells me that in that photograph she can see herself looking into the future, anticipating our long life together. Perhaps some of Ann's interpretation of that photograph is the projection of hindsight, but even so, the photograph puts her in touch with the emotional power of a turning point in her life.

I have another photograph in my album that captures a turning point in my young life. There is no living person in this photo—*just a skeleton!*

Here's the story behind it: I had gone off to military college because of my interest in riding and polo, but had taken an immediate and intense dislike to the regimented life there. Still, I forced myself to buckle down and bear it.

Then, one night near the end of my freshman year, the night before some generals were to arrive from Washington for their annual inspection, an older friend of mine on the polo team, a returned veteran, hatched this incredible scheme: We'd steal the skeleton out of the biology lab and hoist it up the flagpole to greet the arriving brass. I was horrified and fascinated, but much to my own surprise, I couldn't resist. So, in the middle of the night, I found myself stepping gingerly along a narrow ledge five stories up, and then clambering in through an open window to the biology lab. A moment later, I climbed out clutching the skeleton in my arms. The wind had picked up, and the bones were rattling—I was scared, but there was no turning back. Finally down, my partner in crime hoisted those jangling bones up the flagpole just as the sun started to rise.

The chaos that flying skeleton created was a real high for me, a "peak experience," as the expression goes. There was no flag-raising that morning, no reveille. For a moment in time on that tightly regimented campus, I had stopped the normal flow of things.

Although even without a photo, I'd never forget that night, the photograph makes it emotionally real for me in a way that unaided memory never could. When I look at that picture, I can almost viscerally recall the thrills and terrors of that night. And it's the power of those reexperienced feelings that tells me this was more than just a school prank for me—it was a pivotal act of rebellion in my life. I realize that I must have known

that night that I could not remain at that college or any like it, and that I finally had the courage to tell my mother so. I see that this was a critical juncture for me, that at some moment on the ledge outside the biology lab I had understood that there was a limit to the amount of untrammeled authority I could take, and so I had to start looking for a more self-directed way to live my life.

In short, there is an awful lot of personal history—of change and resolution—packed into that snapshot of a skeleton hanging from a flagpole.

To plot long-range trends or themes in a personality or style of life

Rather than isolate pivotal moments in a life, the goal here is to take the long view and look for the attitudes and emotions that bind a life together, to capture its unique shape. Again, the main tool is a chronological series of photographs that revisit the same person or persons over an extended period of time.

In many ways, I find this the most intriguing kind of photo detective work. Like a time-traveler, you can move backward in history, spotting a trait and tracing back in time to its first recorded expression. In this way, for example, you can see how one man I know, a middle-aged comedic actor, was once a clowning teenage schoolboy with

a rose in his mouth and a beanie on his head and, before that, a toddler with a smirk on his face and the undeniable glint of a secret joke in his eye. Or you can see how one woman, who eventually became a nun, had always displayed an awkwardness and discomfort around males, and, going back to her first years of school, a look of otherworldliness in her wide, wondering eyes.

An attractive mother I know put together this sequence of photographs that she calls, "Hey, look at me!"

The series shows that from the start this was a woman who was always putting herself out there, trying to get attention, and succeeding at it. Clearly, she was proud of her appearance even when she was a toddler: Look at that open hand at the side of her naked little body that says, "Hey! Here I am!" Even at this tender age, she exuded the beginnings of body confidence. In the family photo, she is the only one of the three sisters who sits between Daddy's legs, and she has a look of satisfaction—perhaps even triumph—on her smiling face. And then as an adult, there she is again with the same open hand, looking confidently into the camera—"Yes! Here I am at the party!" This woman cheerfully admits now that she almost always got what she wanted in life, often with the help of a man.

Subtler traits can emerge from this line of photoanalysis. I've seen a series of photographs that reveals one man's abiding sense of rootedness: Whether he is pictured in his rocker on his front porch or chatting with friends outside the local post office, the power of his attachment to his environment—his at-homeness—is indisputably there to behold. Similarly, another man's relentless sense of root*lessness* is apparent in a series of photographs he assembled and shared with me: One early photograph shows him as a boy of five earnestly sticking his thumb out like a hitchhiker in front of his family's house, already a wanderer at heart.

Abstract and mythlike life themes can emerge too: A set of twelve photographs encompassing eighteen years in the life of one man tells the dramatic and moving story of a latter-day Prodigal Son, starting with his official U.S. Army photograph on the day he enlisted without his parents' consent, and ending with a photograph of him hugging his father at a railroad station on the day he returned home for the first time in eighteen years.

A woman in her seventies assembled a series of photographs of herself that she calls, "Seeking the Exotic." It creatively connects pictures of herself in such disparate settings as a hothouse at the Brooklyn Botanical Gardens, where, at the age of ten, she stands surrounded by tropical, fly-eating plants, and a monastery in Kathmandu where, at the age of sixty, she stands next to a prayer wheel. Although most of her outward life has been relatively conventional—she married and raised a family in a home less than two miles away from the one she herself grew up in—she has always been fascinated by exotica in nature and culture; and what she could not explore in museum visits and a few, rare vacation trips, she investigated in books. She told me that those six or seven photographs she'd strung together told more about her interior life over the years than all of the rest of the photos in her albums. Those few photos corroborated a significant theme in her life, made it visible both for herself and others.

To uncover subtleties and complexities of an individual's relationship with other people

Photoanalysis can be remarkably effective at this task. Even in the most posed of family portraits, hints to hierarchies in parental favor, to the secret jealousies and affections of siblings, and to the relative cohesiveness of the whole family can be detected.

There are clues in the relative positioning of each family member—who is the focal point of the photograph, who is next to whom. There are clues in the way a head or a body inclines toward or away from other people in the picture. There are clues in the way—and where—people touch or do not touch one another, and in the way a touch is received. There are clues in the expressions on their faces as they regard one another, in the awkwardness or ease of their bodies as they stand or sit beside one another.

There they are all sitting together in front of their summer house in Finland after they fled St. Petersburg. . . . They're sitting together, but so very disconnected, as you can see. My grandfather was the patriarch, and that's my mother sitting to his right in the place where my grandmother should be sitting. He poured all his hopes into my mother. At sixteen, he sent her to Boston to be educated. She graduated from Radcliffe, summa cum laude.

Hundreds of small decisions and reactions are recorded in group photographs of all kinds, not just family photographs. Conscious statements are being made so the pho-

tographer can record them for posterity ("Molly is my best friend!"), but most often, attitudes are being expressed unconsciously but recorded nonetheless.

A man in his mid-fifties uncovered these family pictures taken on the front steps of his first home on a sunny September day in 1936 when he was not quite a year old. Before reading on, try to make sense out of what is going on in these pictures. What is the story here?

Clearly, the mother and father had dressed for the occasion: Note his father's three-piece suit and well-combed hair, his mother's "Sunday" dress, high-heeled shoes, and necklace. His mother's gentleness and loving care are obvious in the way she hunkers down solicitously next to her baby boy, in the gentle smile on her face and in her eyes, and in the way she reaches out and touches him. But equally clear is the father's remoteness from both his wife and child; he appears stuck, awkward, and uncomfortable, on the top step. Yet there is something tender in the expression on his face, a sadness, even, one senses from the hunch of his shoulders and the downward cast of his face, a quality of shame.

Looking back at these photographs some fifty years later, the man who had been a baby boy on that September day was acutely relieved to detect that look of tender shame on his father's face. He realized that his father, who died an alcoholic, had been a drinker even then, inebriated already in the middle of that sunny day, and painfully isolated from his son and wife by both the alcohol and the ineffable sadness that made him consume it.

"I've always known that my father was never a real part of the family, and I guess it always felt like he was rejecting us," the man told me. "But one thing I see in those pictures is how much my father wanted to be closer to us. He doesn't look cold or cruel at all, just lonely, terribly lonely. But he was just too drunk and ashamed and imprisoned inside his head to get any closer to us even then, when I wasn't yet even one year old."

What can be particularly revealing is a pairing or group of persons photographed again and again over a span of time: a beaming couple in courtship snapped at a Christmas dance; the same pair five years later, now married, standing stiffly side-by-side for a group portrait at a family Christmas party; and then two years later, sitting tenderly with their newborn daughter in front of a Christmas tree. A history of a relationship can be thus recorded: from the bloom of romantic love to the strains and disenchantments of early marriage to the warmth and intimacies of settled love. The quality of relationships in marriages, families, and friendships is constantly in flux. And like a film director's storyboard, a series of photographs taken over the years can plot those changes. It can create the outline of a story.

From Picture to Theme to Story Again

As you look at a photograph again and again, prodding yourself with questions about what you see, significant life themes become apparent. For example, when I examined that photograph of the hanging skeleton and realized how fateful that night had been in my life, I found myself wondering about the role rebellion had played throughout my life. One by one, other stories of personal rebellion surfaced in my mind: a rebellion against my mentor at the analytic institute where I trained; a revolt later on against the orthodoxy of traditional psychoanalysis. These newfound stories were both dramatic and revealing: core stories—stories worth telling.

It often happens that when you uncover one core story,

it leads you to another and then another. The stories may be connected to one another in ways that you won't completely understand at first, but then, suddenly, a life theme reveals itself.

The man I mentioned earlier who put together a series of photographs that he called "The Prodigal Son" was able to see the entire arc of defection, profligacy, and redemptive return in his young life only after he had read a collection of universal myths that included "the Prodigal Son." Then, going back to his box of photographs with this mythic theme in mind, he began to assemble his own personal enactment of it, picking out photos and remembering one revealing story after another.

So this process goes, from photograph to story to myth to theme and back to story again. . . .

Asking the Right Questions

Photoanalysis is not an exact science; it is a creative technique, a method of investigation. As in dream analysis, there are no hard-and-fast formulas for interpretation, just clues. You must look at your photographs carefully and systematically, but above all you must look with your imagination.

Is that a look of terror in your eyes as you sit on the see-saw wedged between your brother's legs? Or is that a look of excited contentment?

Try to enter the photograph through your imagination. Try to re-create the feelings that go with that expression on your face.

The procedure of photoanalysis is basically one of careful observation, of asking and answering the right questions. The right questions—those that are resourceful, relevant, and provocative—stimulate your eye and govern the information you obtain.

When I start my analysis of a photograph, I ask myself: What do I feel right now? What moves me the most about the photograph? Is there anything about it that disturbs me?

Then I try to come up with one descriptive word that captures the whole feeling behind the photo.

Then I study each person in the photograph individually. That person is smiling, but *how* is she smiling?

Next I take a blank card and cover one part of a person's body so that I can study another part in isolation. Are the parts harmonious, or are there tensions and inconsistencies? Using this technique, one woman I know looked at a photograph of herself as a child: She found her face earnest, open-eyed, and demure, but when she studied her body, she saw that her hunched shoulders and fidgeting hands expressed shyness and nervousness.

"Those have always been the two sides of me," this woman said. "One part straightforward and calm, the other part so self-conscious I could die. It was fascinating to see it right there in that photograph, back when I wasn't even ten years old."

Studying this photograph, she could take the next step and asked herself, How did this conflict between the two sides of my personality play out in my life? The answer came in one good story after another.

Next, I try to insert myself into the pictured person's skin, try to slip behind his eyes, and I ask myself, What is he feeling? Is he shy? Proud? Angry? Distant? Bored?

Now I look at the photograph for clues to relationships between people. I look to see if they are touching and, if so, how? Are they making eye contact with one another and, if so, how? I try to detect what messages are passing between them. Who stands or sits in a position of dominance? Do I see loving feelings present?

I read each photo from left to right, then up to down. I go over it again and again, each time trying to pick up something I have missed. With repetition, I find myself growing increasingly visually sensitive to the nuances of personality and interpersonal relationships in the photograph.

As you search through your photographs, there are a few techniques I've found that may help you find a fresh perspective on them.

For example, you may want to get yourself a photoanalysis partner, preferably a friend who is not especially knowledgeable about your background or your family. Familiarize your partner with the photoanalysis approach— what to look for, what questions to ask. Then let your partner take the lead, prodding you with fresh, unbiased questions like, "Was your father a melancholy man? He looks so withdrawn from everyone here."

From questions such as these, new perspectives arise, and hidden stories emerge.

You may want to return the favor to your partner, asking questions about and analyzing his photographs.

Another technique is to take those photographs that seem to be brimming with feeling and portents of things to come and imagine that the people in them start moving and speaking like a movie. What would the people in the photograph say to each other? What would motivate them? Don't worry about actual events, let your imagination take charge. Your invented dialogue can lead to a truth of its own, and true stories will follow from that.

Now, take this exercise to the next step—Imagine yourself as you are *now* interacting with the people in the photograph. What do they say to you? You to them?

With the photographs of a lifetime spread out before you on the dining-room table, memory speaks, and the search for the hero of your life continues. . . .

Chapter 5 *Previews of a Life*

———————

Awoman who was having a difficult time inspiring her father to tell Elder Tales to her and her children came to me for advice.

"Dad insists that he doesn't have any interesting stories to tell," she told me. "He says nothing momentous ever happened to him."

The woman went on to say that lately her father had frequently been expressing the feeling that his life has been insignificant.

"And he's so absolutely wrong about that," she continued unhappily. "He's meant more to more people than he realizes."

"Just like George Bailey," I said.

"Who?"

"George Bailey. You know, the character Jimmy Stewart plays in *It's a Wonderful Life*."

For those who don't remember, *It's a Wonderful Life* is director Frank Capra's 1946 film about an "ordinary" man—George Bailey—who despairs that his life has amounted to nothing and who is about to jump off a bridge when a guardian angel stops him and shows him what disasters would have befallen his hometown if he had never lived. At the end of his guided tour of George's past, the angel says, "Strange, isn't it, how a man's life touches so many other lives? When he isn't around, he leaves an awful hole, doesn't he?"

There are some people who consider Capra's film too syrupy to be honestly affecting. Not me. Maybe I am an incurable romantic, but I am deeply moved by this film every time I see it. I suggested to the woman with the recalcitrant father that she get him a cassette of the film to view. She went a step further: She watched it with him.

"About halfway through [the film], I looked across the sofa at Dad, and there were tears in his eyes, which got me going, too, of course," she told me afterward. "There was a lot of sniffling and snorting, but we managed to see that wonderful movie through to the end."

The next day, her father called her to say that he would like to set a date to tell some stories to the family. Clearly, the film had helped him realize that a man's significance could be measured in terms of all the differences—small and large—that he has made in the lives of the people around him. But beyond that, the film provided him with a special perspective from which to begin the review of his own life, to wit, how the world would have been different if he had never existed. It was just the shift in vision that this elder needed to discover the hero of his life. Stories—scores of them—followed.

Life-Review Consciousness

I recommend *It's a Wonderful Life* to everyone who embarks on the Elder Tale Program. It is one of several movies and books I suggest that focus on a character engaged in the life-review process. These works offer intimate glimpses into the different ways people experience looking back over their lives. They can draw us in to what I call "life-review consciousness"—that flow of dreams, memories, and associations unique to this process. They can help us get accustomed to this extraordinary mental territory. They can inspire us.

Just about every elder I know who's watched *It's a Wonderful Life* suddenly finds stories of his own popping to mind. Many of these stories arrive through simple and direct association. The last time I viewed the film, the prom scene where George and Mary start falling in love recalled a courtship scene from my own life: I remembered the time not long after we'd met that I impulsively paid a visit to Ann in Norway and we ended up dancing the night away at the Grand Hotel in Arendal. Other stories may come to mind through thematic associations. Capra's theme that small personal sacrifices and gestures can add up to big differences in the lives of other people summoned up one elder's never-told story about her mother:

When we were still in Poland, my father had a woman working in his notions shop, and she always brought her little boy with her. [The boy] didn't go to school, like many poor children didn't, but somehow he had taught himself to read, and my mother was very impressed with that, so she would lend him books and magazines to read. She was like a little lending library, bringing a book down the stairs to him every few days. . . . [Mother] lost contact with them when we came to America, but many years later—after I was married myself—she got a letter from this little boy, who was now a man living in Switzerland where he had an important job with the International Red Cross. He had tracked Mother down because he wanted to thank her. "You opened up the entire world for me," he said to her in his letter . . .

There is a subtler reason why a good life-review movie like *It's a Wonderful Life* brings stories to mind: It stimulates a feeling for life as a wellspring of stories. Watching this film, filled as it is with small but affecting incidents, we sharpen our insight into what makes a good and revealing story—a story that deserves to be told. The film has a remarkable capacity for awakening Elder Tale-tellers to the power of the *small* story—the little incident with lingering implications, the quiet encounter that stays in the heart. Such stories, of course, often make for the most fascinating Elder Tales.

There is another drama I urge Elder Tale-tellers to see (or see again) for a similar reason, and that is Thornton Wilder's American classic, *Our Town*. The play, a look at turn-of-the-century life in the small New England town of Grover's Corners, is an ode to the splendor in the commonplace events of life. The first act, titled "Daily Life," is just that, a depiction of some townspeople's ordinary pursuits on a May day in 1901. In the third act, Emily, a young woman encountered in the first act who has since died, is permitted to invisibly return from the grave to relive a single day of her life. She chooses her twelfth birthday, but once back and watching her family routinely go through the day, she is appalled by her realization that the living do not appreciate how precious life's small moments are. My heart aches when Emily cries out, "Do any human beings ever realize life as they live it? Every, every minute?"

Although not strictly speaking a life-review drama, *Our Town* serves as a poignant example of the astonishing beauty in the details and textures of daily life. And it is a plea to honor that beauty. The play can be especially instructive when preparing Elder Tale III of the program, "A Day in Your Life," wherein you re-create a single day from your past. Like *It's a Wonderful Life, Our Town* counters that stubborn feeling so many of us have that a story has to be wildly dramatic to be interesting. It inspires the tale-teller to proceed leisurely and with loving care to details.

Incidentally, although there is a fine rendering of this play on film starring Frederic March, I, personally, have been most moved by it in live productions by amateur and high school companies where it is often revived.

The Detours That Get a Story Straight

A retired corporate lawyer named Bill showed me the twelve single-spaced pages he'd written in preparation for telling his life story to his family.

It read like a brief for a lawsuit. All the major events of Bill's life were listed in chronological order; it was an utterly bloodless document. There is little poetry in chronology, no sense of a life in pure data. Although I am the first to acknowledge that there are different styles of life-review consciousness for different people, I felt that Bill had not really entered into this consciousness at all. He wasn't reviewing his life, he was quantifying it. But instead of trying to explain that difference to him, I suggested he take a look at the movie *Avalon*.

Director Barry Levinson's tender family chronicle focuses on an elder named Sam who keeps trying to get his story straight. "I came to America in 1914. . . ." Sam begins again and again throughout the film, only to be interrupted each time by a new memory or stray association, fascinating detours and digressions. Compounding Sam's frustration at not being able to begin at the beginning and proceed in an orderly fashion is a brother of his, a stickler for facts, a man of the "if-you-can't-get-it-exactly-right-don't-bother-to-get-it-at-all" school of reminiscing who is constantly challenging and correcting Sam on details of time and place. But here, also, Levinson gently pokes fun at the relative importance of strict factual accuracy: When Sam starts to regale his family with the story of his father's arrival in America, he sets the pierside scene on a chilly winter day, and we in the audience see the scene that way; but abruptly the stickler brother interrupts—it was *spring*, he insists—and so Sam begins the story again, but this time we see the same scene on a beautiful spring day. Sam's recollection of the day is flexible, adaptable—the heart of it isn't affected by the weather.

Ultimately, *Avalon* tells Sam's life story as a tapestry. Time sequences are interwoven, slipping from one period to another by personal association rather than by chronology. The life that emerges is rich in color and detail; it is conveyed with more feeling and interest than it possibly could be in a story that simply begins at the beginning and proceeds in an orderly fashion.

My elder friend Bill accepted my suggestion and saw *Avalon*.

"So, I gather you think I should be more whimsical," he said to me after he'd seen it. "But you see, I've never been a whimsical man."

"You don't have to be whimsical," I assured him. "Just open to the possibility that stories can come at you from a lot of different directions."

This time I recommended Arthur Miller's autobiography, *Timebends*, to him. This, too, is a work that skips back and forth in time (hence the title), yet Miller's life stories unfold within a tight logic of personal associations and ideas. For example, he recalls a boyhood scene of "running away" from home on his bicycle all the way up to Harlem and calming himself in that neighborhood's utter strangeness; then, in the very next paragraph, he reconstructs a scene in that same neighborhood from some fifty years later when, as a prominent playwright, he lectures at City College and afterward has a disturbing encounter with an African-born cabdriver. It's not just the place, Harlem, that makes these connections in Miller's narrative, it is a common current of feeling about outsiderness and courage that runs from his youth to his middle age.

Bill was deeply impressed by *Timebends*. By the time he finished the book, the manner in which it assembles a mosaic of memories had become part of his own consciousness. Bill concluded that all along his own recollections of the past had been prompted by "disorderly" associations, too, but that he had reflexively "edited out" memories that didn't fit in with his predetermined idea of what a narrative history should be.

"I guess I'd been thinking of my life as a straight line, like an argument," he told me. "It's not, naturally. What connects the stories is that they all happened to me."

Bill had clearly found his way into the realm of life-review consciousness.

Incidentally, *Avalon* has stimulated a number of people I know to think anew about their Elder Tales. The character Sam's relentless attempt to reconcile his golden expectations of life in America with what actually happened to him in this country is a theme that resonates for many immigrant elders; it has led them to core stories of hope and disappointment in their own lives. But most significantly, this film is a paean to storytelling itself. For all of Sam's disappointments, he cherishes the sweetness of his memories, and he knows in his bones that stories are what hold families together. As we watch the television set gradually supplant Sam as the storyteller in his New World family, we know in *our* bones that a terrible mistake is being made.

Dark Shadows, Illuminating Images

Three of the most powerfully affecting life-review movies I know of come to us from Europe: Ingmar Bergman's *Wild Strawberries*, Federico Fellini's *8½*, and Bertrand Tavernier's *A Sunday in the Country*. All three of these masterpieces confront loneliness, melancholy, and the specter of meaninglessness head-on; and all three are poetic testimony to the capacity of a personal life review to achieve self-acceptance and reinvolvement in life.

A Sunday in the Country

I once recommended *A Sunday in the Country* to a friend of mine who was stymied by Elder Tale IV in the program, "Turning Points."

"I'm one of those people who never made big, earth-shattering decisions," she reported to me. "Looking back, it seems like I was always deciding to stay the same, so I really don't have any stories to tell here, do I?"

"I'll bet you do," I said, and that is when I suggested that she take a look at Tavernier's bittersweet film about an aging Impressionist painter who ruminates about life's small pleasures and inevitable disappointments during a Sunday visit from his dutiful son and family, and his lovely, vivacious, self-involved daughter. In one compelling scene, the old father and his daughter sneak off to a garden café straight out of a Renoir painting where, against a backdrop of wine, food, dancing, and sunlight, the daughter asks her father why he has never changed his painting style, even though the rest of the art world has. His reply is moving in its simplicity and candor; he says that his style reflects the way he sees the world, and despite the urgings of his wife and others, he could never see it or paint it otherwise. It is a short and rather undramatic story that he tells his daughter, but it captures something profound about the wisdom of self-acceptance in old age. He is a man without regrets; staying the same is the way he stayed true to himself. This one scene conveys better than any I know the powerful connection that can be made between generations by a simple, honestly told Elder Tale.

My friend was enchanted by the film, especially by the way every scene in it was illuminated by the aging painter's love of natural beauty. And she, too, was moved by the exchange between father and daughter in the café. On reflection, she decided that she had a number of Turning-Point Tales of her own that she wanted to pass on, including one about the time she and her late husband had decided not to move away from the home that they loved.

8½

I recommend Fellini's classic autobiographical film *8½* to everyone embarking on the Elder Tale Program, but especially to those who feel blocked by the critic inside them who protests that all personal memoirs are vain and meaningless.

8½ is about a filmmaker named Guido confronting a creative crisis: Bereft of inspiration, he is unable to come up with a new idea for a film. Stalled mentally, emotionally, even physically (the film begins with him caught in a traffic jam inside a tunnel), Guido begins reviewing his life in a stunning, surreal mix of memories and fantasies that, paradoxically, becomes the content of this, his "new" film. A recurring character in Guido's fantasies is a critic named Daumier, who is the embodiment of all the negativity that haunts every creative person. Toward the end of the film, it is Daumier who raises the ultimate critical question: Why bother telling your life story at all?

"There is no need to leave a film behind you like a deformed footprint of a crippled man," Daumier proclaims. "What a monstrous presumption to believe that others might profit by the squalid catalog of your mistakes. And what good would it do to yourself to piece together the shreds of your life, your vague memories?"

Devastating questions. They express every Elder Tale-Teller's worst doubts. And yet it is by confronting these doubts that Guido finally feels liberated—free to get on with his story and his life.

"Everything is just as it was before," Guido responds ecstatically. "Everything is confused again, but this confusion is *me*! It is because I am as I am, not as I would like to be. I'm not afraid anymore of admitting that I seek and have not yet found. Only this way can I feel alive, only this way can I look into your eyes without shame. . . . Life is a holiday. Let us enjoy it together. Accept me as I am if you can. *It is the only way we really have to find ourselves.*"

Amen. Guido's triumph over his doubts is inspiring, his spirit infectious. I cannot begin to tell you how many elders I know who have come away from this film raring to get on with their stories.

" 'Accept me as I am if you can,' " one woman said, smilingly repeating Guido's line. "I think that's the way I'm going to begin my first Elder Tale."

Wild Strawberries

Every year toward the end of his popular Harvard course, The Human Life Cycle, Professor Erik Erikson would pull down the shades in his lecture hall and show Ingmar Bergman's *Wild Strawberries*.

No case history or psychological report can capture the "overall coherence, the 'gestalt,' of a whole life" as well as this film, Erikson has said. Indeed, *Wild Strawberries* is considered by many—myself among them—to be the most profound, sensitive, and evocative portrayal ever created of an elder in the midst of the life-review process. In the film, we enter the conscious and unconscious life of a septuagenarian Swedish physician named Borg as he sets off on a journey to the university town of Lund where he is to receive an honorary degree for fifty years of dedicated medical practice. Moving from his dreams to his memories to current experiences and back to his dreams again, we see Borg looking back on himself at different stages of life and searching for transcendent themes and meanings. In Erikson's view, this search is one that every elder is involved in, whether or not he is aware of it.

For people engaged in the Elder Tale Program, Bergman's film can be stimulating at many levels, beginning with the way it dramatizes life review as a journey, both literally and metaphorically. Literally, Borg's journey to Lund has much in common with Elder Tale IX, "Sentimental Journeys," wherein the storyteller sets off to a landmark of her past to recollect and tell the life stories that took place there. In the film, we see how evocative such a trip can be—standing outside his family's old summer house, Borg is flooded with dreams and memories from his youth. But it is the metaphor of life review as journey, as a kind of psychic time-traveling through an emotionally loaded landscape, that engages many elders' life-review consciousness. As on any journey, one's sensitivities are heightened. Surprises lurk around every corner.

Wild Strawberries is like a master class in the way personal themes emerge in the process of life review. We watch Borg gradually discovering the way his fastidiousness and self-involvedness have kept him from enjoying the sensuous, loving side of his nature. Such discoveries come to Borg on their own, unsolicited, as one memory leads to another, then that memory to a dream, and that dream to an interaction with the people he meets on his journey to Lund. In a sense, the lesson here is not one of methodology—how to look for themes in your life; rather, it is a lesson in trusting your intuition and recognizing the themes that it gratuitously offers up to you.

In his book *Vital Involvement in Old Age*, Professor Erikson offers a fascinating and lucid account of the themes in Borg's life as they emerge in this film, and how their discovery leads Borg to reinvolvement in his own life. In the final scene of *Wild Strawberries*, Borg connects for the first time with the daughter-in-law who accompanied him on his journey to Lund; it is a moment I would wish for all elders. I can think of no better introduction to life-review consciousness than a viewing of *Wild Strawberries* followed by a reading of Erikson's analysis of it in Chapter 3 of *Vital Involvement in Old Age*.

After doing just that, one elder said to me, "I felt like a genuine student for the first time since college. I'd forgotten what a joy it is to read with a purpose."

This elder's purpose, of course, was to discover the stories of his life so he could tell them to his children and grandchildren. It is a purpose that Frank Capra, Thornton Wilder, Barry Levinson, Arthur Miller, Bertrand Tavernier, Federico Fellini, Ingmar Bergman, and Erik Erikson would all heartily approve of.

At the end of this book, I offer an appendix with reviews of more films and books that have nurtured and intensified the life-review process for me and people I know.

CHAPTER 6 Lebenslauf *Dreams*

"**I** have found that during the last few years I glide rather easily into a twilight world of memories and dreams which are highly personal," Dr. Borg, the seventy-six-year-old protagonist of *Wild Strawberries* notes in his diary. But Borg, a Swedish physician, is quick to deny any interest in interpreting his dreams' meanings: "I have never been particularly enthusiastic about the psychoanalytic theory of dreams as the fulfillment of desires. . . ."

Yet of course Borg's dreams as portrayed in this film classic are brimming with meaning. Not the Freudian-type meaning he disdains, but a more expansive, literary kind of meaning that Erik Erikson has called "life historical" meaning. Borg's are dreams that gather together the threads of a lifetime.

The dreams we dream as elders are often rich with life-historical meaning. They can drop deep into the well of memory, drawing up critical scenes from the past that have escaped our consciousness. They can skip back over our long lives, snatching, say, a vivid encounter from our youth and projecting it alongside a significant moment in middle age, making a brilliant connection between our historical selves. And, by mixing wisdom with fantasy, they can compose personal myths that bear a transcendental message.

In his seminal book *The Forgotten Language*, Erich Fromm states, "We are not only less reasonable and less decent in our dreams, but we are also wiser asleep than when we are awake."

Wiser asleep! I've always liked the sound of that. For elders, with our natural appetite for making sense of our lives, that notion seems to have special applicability. Perhaps the reason that we, like Dr. Borg, glide more easily into the twilight world of highly personal dreams is because we are searching there for wisdom.

Of this much I am certain: Elders who are actively searching for the core stories of their lives dream up a storm of highly personal, meaningful dreams. That makes perfect sense. In dreams, we usually rework and reevaluate our conscious daily experiences; it's as if our dreams take a look back at the events of the previous day and describe and define them anew. Thus, if the most poignant thoughts and feelings of that previous day came from looking at old photographs or reading old letters, from reading a memoir or from visiting an important personal landmark, then these are the images, thoughts, and feelings that will propel and populate our dreams. These dreams go to work on our life stories; they reinterpret our memories. In the Elder Tale Program, such dreams occurred with such frequency that we gave them a name: *lebenslauf* dreams—sweep-of-life dreams.

Dreams, Feelings, and Stories

But what wise secrets can these *lebenslauf* dreams divulge to us?

Hidden and forgotten feelings, for starters. People often tell me that after, say, looking curiously yet benignly at the photograph of an old friend or relative in the afternoon, they go to bed that night and dream about the pictured person with intense and surprising emotions.

"I found a photograph of myself and a girl I knew briefly in Paris right after the war," a World War II veteran named Arthur told me. "It was taken by one of those street photographers who snapped your picture and then gave you a ticket so you could redeem it later. I remembered that I'd liked the girl, although I'd forgotten her name. . . . Well, in my dream that night, I was kissing her hair, and I swear I could smell it in my sleep. It was so woman-sweet . . . I was young

and unattached, the war was over, and I was in Paris. . . .
I'd actually forgotten what a passionate young man I'd been
back then."

Then, as so often happens after reconnecting with an
intense emotion in a dream, waking memories followed that
were prompted by those awakened feelings. Suddenly, Arthur found himself flooded with memories of himself in his
twenties and early thirties when he had been a passionate,
brash, and somewhat reckless young man. In the dream, he
had rediscovered his passionate self, a self that had become
lost or denied or perhaps simply tired out over the course
of time. But now scene after scene of this self flashed in his
mind, not just scenes of love, but scenes of explosive an-
ger too.

I should note that, at least in this case, these stories
emerged without further thought or analysis. They all sprang
directly from the powerful feeling that Arthur carried back
from his dream. Ultimately, feeling is always the source of
memory; it's what propels it into our consciousness. If Arthur had not come to identify with his once-passionate self,
if he had not in some way reexperienced those feelings, a
treasury of stories would probably have been lost to him.
Even if he had somehow come across the stories in another
way—say, via an old letter—but had not emotionally connected with them, the stories would not have amounted to
much either to him or to whomever he told them to. If he
had not recalled in his heart what he had felt for that Pari-
sian girl or how he had felt in general during that period of
his life, the story of that encounter would have been pale,
insignificant, and unrevealing. Feelings are the power of the
story as well as the source of the memory.

Lebenslauf dreams may also reveal meanings through
the associations they make within the dream and the associations our awake selves make with them.

Dreams are notorious for "irrationally" combining elements of a person's life. Awakening, the dreamer finds that
in his dream he'd been the "wrong" age at the "wrong"
time, with the "wrong" people in the "wrong" place, that

the interior of the dream scene had been New York, but once he walked outside, it was obviously Martha's Vineyard.

These odd combinings are irrational, to be sure, but the suspension of logic and reason is precisely a dream's greatest asset. Instead of regarding them as confusions, we should ask ourselves what *wisdom* lurking in our sleep matched up those seemingly unrelated elements of our life? Trying to answer that question can lead us to hidden life themes and, very likely, to more and more astonishing stories.

An elder named Nat reported a dream he had that took place at the summer house of his youth on Lake Michigan; but instead of being there with his parents and brother, he was there with his former business partner, the man with whom he had opened his first haberdashery at the age of thirty-one. In the dream, both Nat and his partner seemed much younger. Little seemed to happen: They built a campfire together and fried some steaks over it.

Awake, Nat wondered about this strange juxtaposition. He associated that summer house with the happiest days of his youth, yet all he associated with his former business partner was bitterness and pain: After five years of building a shop together, the partner had abruptly backed out and gone into business with someone else in another town. Nat thought about that campfire in his dream: Building it had been accompanied by a feeling of camaraderie and adventure; the fire itself had been dazzling; and those steaks had only tasted more delicious for all the work it took to get the cook-fire going.

That was it! Nat suddenly saw the connection that the dream had made for him: Building that fire was very much the way it had been to build that business together—the camaraderie, the adventure, the pride, the satisfaction in the fruits of their labor. He had actually forgotten all about those pleasures; he'd buried them under the pain of his partner's defection and then left them there.

Why the summer house? Those were sunny, golden times in Nat's life, just as the first years of building the haberdashery had been. This led Nat to another association: Those summers on Lake Michigan had ultimately been lost too; Nat's family had had to give up their summer house in the Depression.

Nat considered the ebb and flow of blissful hope and bitter loss in his life; they seemed like recurring themes. But he now decided that as he'd been going about collecting the stories of his life, he'd been neglecting the thread of satisfaction and hope, that he'd been allowing his low points to eclipse his high points. Now, several buried and forgotten stories of high points from various stages of his life began to come back to him, stories that gave more balance and scope to the sweep of his life. And it all started with a dream about building a campfire.

Often, *lebenslauf* dreams are ignited by story preparation and storytelling itself. A man named Arnold was involved in Elder Tale VII of our program: Coming up with a fitting title for the "novel of his life" and telling the stories that made it so. After much discussion with friends, Arnold decided on the title "The Man Who Always Tried Again."

Arnold's father had frequently used the expression, "If at first you don't succeed, try, try again," especially when coaching his son in batting practice when he would sometimes vary the expression to "Swing, swing again." The message had stuck with Arnold long after his father's death—killed in an automobile accident when Arnold was still a boy—and Arnold had many stories to tell to substantiate this title: a story about his repeated rebuffs but finally successful attempt to get into Cornell University; a story about his relentless pursuit of the woman who ultimately became his wife, wooing her away from another college baseball player; a story about building his own landscape-design business in difficult times.

The night after telling these "The Man Who Always Tried Again" stories to his children and grandchildren, Arnold had a vivid dream about a baseball game:

I was sitting on an old wooden bench in the dugout, watching our team get murdered. We couldn't get a hit for anything. The coach tells me to go out and hit a single, but I'm unable to move. I feel glued to the bench. My heart begins to beat fast and loud; you can hear the echo all over the park. I'm thinking, everyone must know how scared I am. . . . Finally, I get myself to the batter's box, but they've brought in a relief pitcher, a very menacing-looking guy who looks vaguely familiar to me. Well, he fires one straight at me, almost hits me. Same with the next; it's like he's trying to kill me. As he winds up for the third pitch, everything becomes frozen in time. I hear a voice—"Swing. Swing." I jump back from the plate and swing at it with all my might. From the sound of the crack, I know I've hit more than a single. I notice my wife's old boyfriend as I round first base, but what really catches my eye is the pitcher—he's having a fit, jumping up and down, screaming his lungs out. But I can't make out what he's screaming—all I hear is the cheering.

What an extraordinary, affirmative dream! But there is more to it. Thinking about the dream later, Arnold finally "recognized" that relief pitcher: It was his stepfather, the alcoholic and cruel man who had replaced his own, encouraging father. The moment Arnold associated the relief pitcher of his dream with his stepfather, he recalled an incident from his youth that he hadn't thought of in decades:

My stepfather was not just mean; he was dangerous and abusive, especially when drunk. I remember now the last time he tried to pull me out of bed and beat me—I was still in high school. He came home roaring drunk, charged into my bedroom, but I got away from his grip as he tried to punch me. . . . The next evening I took my baseball bat down to dinner with me and told him that if he ever tried to beat me again, I'd take my bat and bash his brains out while he was sleeping. . . . He never laid a hand on me after that.

Again, from a somewhat simple and fanciful dream, a true and trenchant story emerged that gave deeper meaning to a life theme: Arnold was more than simply a man who kept trying and trying again—he was a man who had the courage to stand up for himself against formidable danger.

Lebenslauf dreams lead us in any number of directions to any number of stories. They may connect events in different stages of our life with a transcending theme. They may ferret out hidden feelings in a relationship. They may identify a high point, low point, or turning point in our life history. They may disclose a hidden hope or a forgotten realization. They might resolve an unfinished story or add an epilogue to a story we've told the day before. And they might cast an old story in a new perspective, one that is driven by feelings that were uncovered in the dream.

But I would be remiss if I stopped here, for *lebenslauf* dreams can do more than disclose stories for us to tell— they frequently provide us with a personal catharsis and renewal. After dreaming about his long-lost passionate young self, Arthur not only uncovered forgotten stories, he brought some of that old feeling back into his life. Once he reexperienced that old emotion, some of it remained with him.

"That dream was me and, hell, I'm still me," Arthur announced. "I'm not saying I'm about to go out and run after women at my age, but I don't feel like forgetting what I feel about them either. In fact, it seems to me I still have strong feelings about all sorts of things."

Similarly, Nat found himself feeling less generally bitter and melancholy after his "campfire" dream. It had helped release him from a one-sided perspective on his life. Seeing the sweep of his life in its fullness was a tremendous relief to him.

In *Wild Strawberries*, Dr. Borg's series of *lebenslauf* dreams start him on the path of recovery from his lack of involvement with life, a process that culminates in Borg's reconciliation with his daughter-in-law, his son, his housekeeper, and, ultimately, his own alienated self. Like good therapy, it made him feel both more alive and more at peace with himself.

Lebenslauf *Dream Analysis*

Like Dr. Borg, I have never approved of dream analysis that starts with its conclusions, that approaches a dream with a set of assumptions about precisely what they can and cannot reveal or what dream images can and cannot symbolize. For me, the only interpretations that are relevant in *lebenslauf* dream analysis are *personal* associations—associations with the events in one's own history and with one's own personal symbols. For example, in Arnold's dream, baseball stands above all else for his relationship with his natural father; in a sense, baseball stands for baseball, the game father and son played and trained for together. Next, Arnold's role in this dream ball game stands for his will, his personal faith in success through perseverance and in overcoming danger through courage. And only then, *if at all*, do I believe that those bats and balls have any of the sexual symbolic significance that a Freudian analyst would be so quick to assign.

The first step in *lebenslauf* dream analysis is to record the dream and all the personal associations and stories that spring from it. Dreams have a tendency to slip away fast in their flight from consciousness, so get them down as quickly as you can upon awakening. It's convenient to have a notebook and pen handy on your bedside table or, better yet, a small, memo-type tape recorder. Don't be meticulous about pinning down the dream events in the "right" order or getting the details exactly straight. Get your dream down sloppily, if that's the way it comes back to you. Most important is to capture the dream's basic feel and sense. Details are significant, of course, but what you recollect about the dream can be as relevant as the dream itself: Your immediate reconstruction of your dream represents your reflex interpretation of it, your first attempt to make sense of it. It sometimes helps to close your eyes and see if you can drift back into a dreamy state: You may yet be able to snag images from the dream that are still floating close to consciousness. Dream feelings, too, may still be lurking close to the surface.

Next, move on directly to any personal stories that follow *without reflection* from the dream and get those down fast too. Only after this is done should you proceed with a more methodical examination of your dream, searching deliberately for your personal associations with it.

Below are a series of questions to ask yourself that we found useful for prying personal associations, meanings, and stories out of a *lebenslauf* dream. These are just guidelines; don't feel compelled to ask them all. And be assured, there are no "right" associations or meanings, just some that seem to ring truer than others—and you are the only one who can judge that. Obviously, a single image, dream character, or plot turn can have more than one association; in fact one association will usually lead to another and yet another. Nat's chain of associations from his "campfire" dream demonstrates this well: He moved from the campfire to the joy of building his haberdashery business to the pain of loss of his partner to the pain of loss of his family's summer house and then back to all the joy, hope, and satisfaction that had preceded his losses. In general, you should try to be as loose as you can in your associations; don't dismiss any of them out of hand for being too "way out." But by the same token, there is not necessarily any virtue in elaborate or complex associations; often the simplest are the most revealing.

The Questions

1. What experience triggered your lebenslauf *dream?*

Almost invariably, some event, encounter, thought, or remembrance from the day before triggered your dream: a photograph you looked at, a story you told, a reminiscing conversation you had with a friend, personal associations you had with a book you read or film you saw. Trace your way back from your dream to this triggering experience and then try to discover what personal associations linked the dream to the experience.

2. What was your first reaction to the dream?

On awakening, were you anxious, disoriented, elated, frightened, aroused, relieved? Did you feel younger than you usually feel? Wiser? More connected to your life?

Did you want to forget the dream? Is there something in the dream that you wanted to keep? A feeling that you wanted to carry out of the dream into your waking life?

Can you describe to yourself why the dream made you feel as it did? Can you determine which elements of the dream had the strongest emotional impact on you? What associations do you have with these feelings? What real events in your life have made you feel this way in the past?

3. How would you describe the characters in your dream, including yourself?

Are they—you—in or out of control? Active or passive? At odds with the others in the dream or in harmony with them?

What do these characters feel? Do feelings change in the dream, say, from fearful to confident? What causes them to change?

Could any one of the characters in your dream be more than one real person in your life? If so, what characteristic do those people have in common that they could coexist in one dream character?

Could you have been more than one of the characters in your dream? Parts of different characters? Do any stories come to mind that dramatize these different aspects of yourself?

Describe how each character moved the action of the dream or reacted to the action of the dream. Are there any discrepancies between feelings and actions? Is there, for example, an obvious danger without any feeling of fear?

4. Did different periods or stages of your life coincide in your dream?

Did your dream flow from one period of your life to another? If so, what seemed to connect them?

Were you the "wrong" age for the period in your life that you dreamed about? Were you your present age, revisiting your past? How did your present self feel about your past self? Again, look for the themes that transcend your different historical selves: What makes all these selves *you?*

5. *What made you feel this was a* lebenslauf *dream?*
    Why is this a dream that only you could have dreamed?
    How did it put you in touch with the sweep of your life?
    What core stories derive directly from this dream?

Indeed, we are wiser asleep. *Lebenslauf* dreams can lead the way to the most revealing stories of our lives.

PART III

The Elder Tale Program

Anne Fanning

"Let me start with my generation—with the grandparents out there. You are our living link to the past. Tell your grandchildren the story of the struggles waged, at home and abroad. Of sacrifices freely made for freedom's sake. And tell them your own story as well—because every American has a story to tell."
—PRESIDENT GEORGE BUSH
State of the Union Address, 1990

"Listening children know stories are *there*. When their elders sit and begin, children are just waiting and hoping for one to come out, like a mouse from a hole."
—EUDORA WELTY
One Writer's Beginnings

INTRODUCTION: *Overcoming Resistance*

Now it is time to get down to business—to tell these stories of your life to your family. And family may include extended family members and close friends. It's up to you. What follows is a ten-step program that has been designed to bring out entertaining, moving, and revealing stories in a sequence that is comfortable for both you and your listeners. Starting with easily accessible "Snapshot" stories of your life, you move by degrees to deeper and more intimate stories—the stories that describe the most significant points of your life and evoke its major themes.

But no part of this program is chiseled in stone. The Elder Tale Program is a menu from which you can pick and choose as you will, as feels right for you. This is not a set of rules. There is no required order. I certainly don't expect everyone to do all ten tales. For one person, Elder Tale V, "High Points and Low Points," may draw out his most intimate and dramatic core stories, while Elder Tale VI, "Epiphanies and Lessons," may not suggest a single story; and for another person, it could easily be the other way around. You will probably want to look over the entire program before you begin to see what options lie ahead. If an idea or setup in the program helps you to produce stories that tell who you are and what your life has been about, then it's right. If it doesn't, keep looking, because I can assure you that some part of the program will; it has for everyone I know who has tried it.

Give each suggested type of Elder Tale time to develop in your mind. Perhaps Elder Tale VIII, "Telegrams and Epitaphs," may not mean anything to you when you first read it over, but some days later while looking at a photograph

*old friends
today; like it
was only yesterday
our disjointed
conversation
have more
meaning, more
intimacy then a
"in depth" conversation*

*Kathie's party
Our New Year
Kirby Xmases*

or reading a book, a story that fits that category perfectly will suddenly pop into your head. Similarly, think of Elder Tale–Telling as a process that can potentially go on and on; it certainly does not have to end after Elder Tale X. Rituals that work tend to perpetuate themselves.

A Family Ritual

As I've said from the start, it is important to think of Elder Tale–Telling as a ritual. That means making it into an event that is planned, celebrated, and honored, just as any other family ritual is, say, Thanksgiving, a bar mitzvah, Mother's Day, or Christmas dinner. Elder Tale–Telling isn't likely to simply happen on its own in this day and age; that's why we had to reinvent it. So like any other family ritual, a date has to be set, people invited, preparations made.

In addition to the tale-teller, one member of the family should assume a leadership role in making this ritual happen. It will be up to this person to schedule the event and issue invitations, and it will probably fall to him or her to help the tale-teller with any preparations needed, say, props. Also, this person should assign someone to be in charge of recording the event, either on audiotape or videotape (some hints on this below).

Together with the tale-teller, this family member will set the ritual going, get people seated and ready to listen. And once started, it will be his or her responsibility to be the most active listener, to prod the teller with questions to keep stories coming or to bring a story back on track after a long digression. His questions will help set the tone for the event, make sure that it is both fun and respectful, free yet focused.

Many families schedule their first Elder Tale–Telling as part of a traditional family event—say, a birthday or anniversary, Christmas, Easter Sunday, Mother's Day, or Thanksgiving. These are days when the extended family probably gets together anyhow, and so it seems natural to add this new ritual to the existing one. In fact, these holidays are likely to be ones that have lost much of their original ritual meanings anyhow (How many Thanksgiving celebrations degenerate into TV football-viewing sessions?), and so the Tale-Telling will naturally fill this ritual void. In my experience, it does not take long for a family to recognize this; they quickly appreciate that they have come together for a genuine purpose rather than to mindlessly fulfill a family duty. Scheduling successive Elder Tale–Telling sessions is much easier: The ice has been broken; people know why they are coming, and they look forward to it.

A word about getting the session started after everyone is comfortably seated around the elder: People will want to chat for a while before the stories "officially" begin. Let them; it puts everyone more at ease. Then, after several minutes, someone can make an introduction, like, "Mom's going to tell us some stories about herself today. Let's listen." That's usually all it takes.

How long does a storytelling session last, and when do you know it is over?

Again, there are no rules, just some averages. Most Tale-tellers and their families feel comfortable with about an hour of stories. The inevitable questions and answers that follow will usually extend this another half hour or so.

Like any ritual, Elder Tale–Telling needs a special gesture or celebration to give it closure. Throughout the program, I offer some suggestions: a drink, a toast, a song, hands-around-a-circle. I think the form the ending celebration takes should be the elder's choice. For the first session, it probably should be arranged ahead of time.

Incidentally, ending celebration or not, the stories don't seem to stop. In most families, it is at this "end" point that other family members start to tell their own stories in response to the ones the elder has told. And these stories seem to continue on, in the car ride home, in bed that night, on the phone the next day. Stories beget stories.

I should note here that a great many extended families have trouble bringing their far-flung members together more than once or twice a year, and that is a long time between Elder Tale–Telling sessions. Some families continue more regularly in smaller groups consisting of the family members who live closest to the elder. They then mail a video of these sessions to the others. One elder I know, an inveterate radio lover, continues between personal sessions by preparing what he calls his monthly "radio show" of stories on audiotape that he sends to his family members all over the country. And a woman I know has developed what she calls her "Traveling Elder Tale Kit"—a constantly changing scrapbook of photographs and other memorabilia that she carries with her on her annual circuit of visits to her children and grandchildren.

It's a Take

Even though it may give added "stage fright" to some elders at first, I always think it's a very good idea to record Elder Tale sessions on videotape. As with any good book or movie, you and your family will want to see it again . . . and again. I know some families who start off each new Elder Tale session by viewing parts of the last one. It's fun, it gets the ball rolling again, and it makes everyone feel part of this "family production." Further, the videotapes serve as a permanent record for your family members of the future; the tapes become the library of your family's oral-visual history. Finally, as I've noted above, these videos can be sent to family members who are unable to attend sessions themselves.

There are advantages to having an operator behind the camera all the time—he can zoom in for close-ups of, say, a photograph that the elder is referring to, and he can pan the "audience" for reaction shots. But videoing an hourlong session is not only tiring work, it can prevent the camera operator from participating fully in the proceedings; for example, it's not easy to ask questions while holding a camera.

The alternative chosen by most families is to set up the video camera on a tripod, adjust the focus, frame your subject—the Tale-Teller—turn on the camera, and leave it alone except to reload tapes.

Here is a check list for whoever is in charge of recording the session:

- Purchase new, good-quality videocassettes. Using poor quality or used tapes can result in recordings with picture and/or sound defects.

- If you have a choice between power from a battery or from an outlet, choose the latter. With AC power, you do not have to worry about batteries dying in the middle of a session. If you do use battery power—say, out of doors—make sure that you have fully charged batteries.

- If you are unfamiliar with the camera being used, check it out thoroughly beforehand. You can put a serious damper on a session by stopping to figure out technical details after it has begun.

- Whether indoors or out, pay close attention to light levels and to ambient sound. Light that is too harsh will produce a washed-out picture as well as a squinting storyteller. A dimly lit area can produce a muddy image. As to ambient sounds, an occasional cricket chirp or telephone ring is acceptable, but the constant rumble of nearby traffic or too much wind can muddle the sound quality.

- For best results, set up the video camera between three and four feet away from the tale-teller. Make sure your framing allows enough room for him or her to move around a bit without disappearing from the picture.

- Always test your equipment before the session begins to make sure everything is working. In reviewing your test sample, look carefully at the lighting and listen closely to sound quality; make sure you can clearly hear everything the Tale-Teller says.

Last-Chance Excuses

There are people, elders and children alike, who love the "idea" of Elder Tale–Telling but come up with all kinds of resistances and excuses for why it's not for them. I've tried to address most of these resistances already, especially those that derive from the feeling that your life is not important enough to merit all this fuss; I trust there is no one who has come this far with me who still harbors that ridiculous notion.

But there still remain many hesitancies and questions that I should finally put to rest here.

Foremost among these is the protest: *"This is all well and good for some people, but I'm not a storyteller!"*

Or, "I just don't have the gift of gab."

Or, "I always run out of things to say."

To all of which I reply, "I'll bet you anything that you'll be better at this than you think—*far better*!"

The main reason I can say that with such confidence is because I've seen it happen again and again. Every elder has interesting stories to tell—that's a fact. Some just need clues on how to get them out, and that is precisely what this program provides.

Still, many elders remain worried about their "performance."

"I don't like being put on the spot," they tell me. "I'll just get nervous with everybody looking at me and waiting for me to say something wonderful."

"That's great!" I reply. "The spotlight *is* on you! You *are* the star of the hour!"

The trick is to take your nervousness and use it to propel your story. That nervousness is energy; it is excitement. The element of "stage fright" will dissipate as soon as the storytelling begins; at that point, you will realize just how well prepared you are. Further, you will discover how to use the props at hand—the photographs and souvenirs—to shift some of the focus away from yourself. Finally, like any performer, you will feel your nervousness being transformed into confident energy as soon as you see the encouraging faces of your family gathered around you—as you win over your audience.

I've had some elders tell me that they don't want to tell their life stories because they don't completely trust their memories. They say they wouldn't feel right about passing on stories to their children and grandchildren that they aren't sure are accurate.

"A lot of my memories kind of have a life of their own," a man in his eighties told me. "I mean, I know when I was a kid, I took a canoe trip down the Missouri River, but sometimes I remember meeting up with some Indians along the way and other times I think that Indian part was something that happened to my stepbrother, not to me. What do I do with a story like that?"

Good question. In fact, it is the kind of question that memoirists and autobiographers have always grappled with. To answer it, one has to try to draw some distinctions, beginning with which facts one considers essential to conveying the truth of one's life and which not. Because the bare facts—the precise whats, whens, and wheres—are not the most important element of Elder Tale–Telling. The personal qualities of experience are. We're all aware that two people attending the same party can come home from it with two entirely different versions of what happened at that party. The party was the same, each person's experience of it was different. A person's life stories should be his version of how he experienced his life.

Still, did my friend meet up with those Indians on his canoe trip or not? And if he's not sure, should he be telling that story to his children and grandchildren?

Well, if he cannot verify these facts by asking someone else or by looking in his diaries or letters, I think he has to ask himself this question: Does the story I seem to remember—Indians and all—feel true to the quality of my life at that time and in that place? Does it evoke life along the Missouri River in the first decades of this century as I experienced it as a boy?

And if the answer to that question is yes, I think he should tell the story as his own and not have a single worry about it. To my mind, the story you remember—even if it's been elaborated on over the years—is the story that counts. It may mix in some wishes and dreams with the bald facts, but those wishes and dreams tell as much about who you are as the facts alone. In his preface to *Inventing the Truth*, the editor, William Zinsser, writes that the essays in that book demonstrate how a variety of memoirists have "sorted out their memories and their emotions and arrived at a *version* of their past that they *felt* was true."

That is all any listener can ask of an Elder Tale–Teller.

Perhaps the biggest block of resistance to telling life stories is the fear of unleashing upsetting feelings.

"I'm too old to start analyzing myself," people say to me.

To which I answer, "You don't have to analyze anything. You just have to tell the stories that tell who you are."

As a psychotherapist, I can assure them there is a big difference between that and self-analysis. Our purpose in Elder Tale–Telling is to see a life as a whole, to report it as it is, not to attempt to take it apart or to change it. Inherent to this approach is an attitude of acceptance: "My life is what it is. And here are its stories."

But, of course, it is never quite as simple as that. Many people have a fear of revealing too much about themselves, of guilty secrets slipping out. Others are frightened of confronting too many of their life's losses, of becoming overwhelmed by their regrets.

First, let me say that we've set up the Elder Tale Program so that potentially upsetting stories are kept at bay for quite some time. Only after the storytelling has become a regular family communication do such stories become a possibility. And rest assured that no one is ever forced to tell any story or to answer any question that she does not want to. No cross-examination, not even gentle pestering, is allowed. That's a fundamental ground rule of this program.

But I wouldn't presume to say that secrets never slip

out or regrets are never confronted in the course of telling the stories of your life. Of course that sometimes happens, and when it does, upsetting feelings surface. Few people can tell their life stories without experiencing a whole gamut of emotions, without going from laughter to tears and back again. As well it should be. The real shame would be a lifetime in stories that left you unmoved.

And the truth is, sharing these secrets and regrets is invariably healing. I can say that with assurance after seeing so many families go through this process. Guilts and sorrows and regrets that festered in the dark for so long surface in the air and suddenly lose their power to hurt. Seen in the context of a whole lifetime of stories, they no longer overwhelm you. You see them as part of your life, not the whole of it.

Elders' children and grandchildren sometimes tell me that they are afraid this program will promote a morbid frame of mind.

"Isn't it like asking my father to write his own eulogy?" one man asked me. "Like saying to him, 'The end is just around the corner, so let's hear your stories before it's too late'?"

All I can reply is that not a single elder I know has found this program in the least morbid. Sure, it made them focus on the fact that they were in the last stage of their life (something they never doubted anyhow), but once they were into the process of gathering and telling their life stories, they were exhilarated, not depressed.

No more excuses. Let's begin.

Elder Tale I: *Snapshots from Your Youth*

—————

For this first adventure in Elder Tale–Telling, select a dozen photographs from your youth— from when you were still living at home with your parents—and tell stories suggested by these photographs. If you wish, you can include several photos of your parents or grandparents before you were born.

First Set a Date

Before you even begin looking through your photos, choose a date with your children for the Tale-Telling itself. Don't make it too soon—you need a little time to prepare. But don't set it for too far off, either—that's how nervousness can build and excuses can crop up. Three to six weeks from today is a good range. Incidentally, you may want to limit this first session to a small group of listeners—not your entire extended family. You can work up to larger groups as you go along—it's your choice.

Choosing Your Photographs

You'll probably start by looking in your family albums, but don't neglect those old shoeboxes stuffed with loose photos—the ones that never found their way into your albums. These "overlooked" photos can often surprise you with their power to evoke long-forgotten stories.

Don't feel that you have to look through every photograph you own at this point. For one thing, you are only looking for photos of your young life.

And don't attempt to analyze your photographs for subtle meanings or currents this time: You are only looking for those pictures that seem to have stories leaping right out of them, pictures that suggest a story the moment you look at them.

That's my dog, Petey. . . . You see, one day he chased a pigeon off our back porch, he thought he could fly, and he landed on the concrete three floors below. Petey lost the use of his back legs, and the vet wanted to put him to sleep, but my mother said no, it would kill me. She had this idea she'd make him this thing with wheels on it, a sling chariot, and she did, and it worked too. He could run and he even got into dogfights . . .

The photo and story were an obvious "keeper" for a grandmother named Marta. She passed over scores of other photographs before stopping at this one, because none of those photos said anything special to her: Either no stories came to mind, or if they did, the stories did not have a powerful-enough feeling attached to them.

Your immediate emotional response to a photograph is

what tells you if the story is one you should consider telling. A smile, a rush of sentiment, a spontaneous "Oh God, whatever happened to *him*?"—These are all clues that there is a story there you might want to tell.

"Most of them are just pictures, you know," Marta told me. "They didn't jump out at me."

But the photo of her and her dog did more than just "jump"—it skipped Marta's mind to another story.

I suddenly remembered. . . . This picture was in the newspaper because some woman had seen me and Petey and my mother in the park and tried to have us arrested for cruelty to animals. I remember my mother telling this woman to go to hell, which at the time was unheard of in Golden Gate Park. . . . Anyway, then the woman wanted my mother arrested for that too. . . . My mother was wild that way, always spoke right out. Everybody thought she was crazy, I guess, but she was fearless. . . .

At times you will amaze yourself by details of memory that suddenly present themselves to you. An elder named Don remembers coming upon this snapshot of his tenth birthday party and suddenly remembering the gift given to him by one of his guests and how important that gift figured in his life.

His name was Henry White, the garbageman's son, and he gave me a rabbit's foot key chain that I wore on my belt for the whole next year. Never missed a day. I remember I was absolutely sure that rabbit's foot was going to make me win the Memorial Day bike race that year. . . ."

Above all, a tellable story is one that

resonates for you. It may appear small to you in some ways—merely the story of a rabbit's foot that seemed to bring good luck—but if the story has a special emotional charge for you, if, say, you can remember, as Don did, that feeling of invincibility when he touched that rabbit's foot as he raced to the finish line on his bicycle, then that story is eminently tellable. Because it tells a great deal about this boy of ten. It told how he felt about himself, what mattered to him, and what he thought was magical in the world.

These are the things your children and grandchildren want to know about you. These are the stories they want to hear.

Often a photograph will suggest an irresistible moment of feeling or atmosphere, but not a narrative story. This can be well worth telling too. The stories here need not be a dramatic sequence of events; they can be more akin to a poem, evoking the sense of a time and place, the feelings of a long-ago moment.

Here are a few lines excerpted from one elder's "Snapshot" tale that was suggested by a photo of her standing in front of her grandfather's barn:

There was a special kind of a daydream I'd have lying in the hayloft of my grandfather's barn. I'd fix my eyes on a shaft of bright sunlight coming through a space between the barn boards. Stare at the floating hay dust until I'd put myself into kind of a trance. And then I'd dream about my future. The sky

was the limit in those daydreams. Lying in my grandfather's hayloft, I could imagine becoming the queen of England. . . .

Remember, don't be alarmed or upset when you cannot remember anyone or anything in a particular photograph. Just pass it by. This is a search for special stories, not a memory test.

When you have selected twenty or so photographs, winnow them down to a *dozen* of your favorites.

Aim for variety—say, a photo of you with your best friend in fourth grade followed by one taken during the first summer vacation you spent alone at your grandparents' farm, then one of you and your sister followed by one of your father tossing horseshoes at the company picnic. Again, you need not make an effort to analyze these photos for hidden meanings or to look for connections between your stories at this point. Right now, you are just picking out slices of your life to share.

Preparation

Now that you've settled on your dozen photos, arrange them in any order you like (it does not have to be chronological order) and note down the salient aspects of each photo:

- The *names* of the people in the photo

- *Where* and about *when* it was taken (to the best of your recollection)

- Who took the photo? (If you can remember)

- Any *special circumstances* you can remember surrounding the taking of the photo—for example, if it was a trip or other special occasion

- A single line or a few code words to describe each story that a photograph suggests to you, for example, "Rabbit's foot—bike race" or "Petey and Mom's arrest."

Keep these notes as brief as possible. You may want to put them on a three-by-five card or on a Post-it sheet that you can attach to the back of the photograph.

These are your "crib notes." You may never have to take a look at them when you tell your stories, but just in case in the rush of the moment some detail slips your mind, the notes are there to remind you. But these notes should not limit your stories—new thoughts, feelings, even new stories, are very likely to occur to you when it's Tale-Telling time.

Some people like to practice telling their stories by themselves—sort of a rehearsal. That's fine, if it makes you comfortable, but it's not necessary. You don't want to over-rehearse; that can take some of the spontaneity out of your actual "performance." As you get used to telling your stories, you will probably find yourself wanting less time for preparation and rehearsal.

Setting the Scene

Decide with your family on the time of the appointed day when you will tell your story—for example, after dinner, before coffee and dessert.

Also work out with your family where you are going to do it. It should be in a setting where everybody can sit comfortably and where it is easy to show photographs and pass them around. It's also a good idea to have a coffee table handy for spreading out photos.

Telling the Tale

"We've asked Grandma to tell us some stories about her childhood today."

And so the first story begins.

You may wish to start with the facts—the who, what, and where—and then move on to your story or stories.

Let each story run as long as feels right and natural. If,

after a couple of minutes, you've said all you feel like saying about a particular photograph, move on to the next. But if the photo sets off a train of stories, let them roll from one to the next. Marta's story about her dog led naturally to one about her mother, and then, as she was talking about her mother's fearlessness, to yet another:

She was a fearless champion of the underdog. . . . Like I remember the day she took me on a bus to the Tanfarn Race Track in Northern California to find out what had happened to Shizue, a student of hers. . . . Shizue and her family had been taken by the federal government to an internment camp. . . . I remember the barbed wire all around the track, and there were soldiers posted at regular intervals with rifles and drawn bayonets. . . . Shizue's father didn't want to see us at first, because of the deep shame of it. My mother began to cry. Then he came out, saying that the tears of a friend were more important than his shame. My mother grabbed hold of the fence, trying to reach him, and she moved so suddenly, the soldier nearest her broke his stance and pointed his rifle at my mother, but my mother wouldn't let go. She said "Marta, don't ever forget this—this is America."

Stories within stories, suggested by a single photograph.

It's interesting to think about what values are being transmitted on the "Me & Petey" stories, what wisdom might be passed from one generation to another by the telling of them. To me, these are stories that speak loudly about a reverence for life, be it human or animal, as well as about justice and fair play. They also speak of another kind of integrity, the kind that is loyal to friends and loved ones and will not capitulate to authority. They are the stories of a woman who did things her way even if it was not the accepted way. There's wisdom there for any listener.

Often, your listeners will have questions for you, wanting to know something that has special significance for them. For example, one of Marta's sons asked, "Weren't you always terrified that Grandma would do something so dangerous that she would get herself hurt or killed?"

It's best if these questions wait until after you have finished offering everything you have to say about a particular photograph. Also, remember the basic rule: *You don't have to feel obligated to answer any question that might make you feel uncomfortable for whatever reason.*

There's a chance you will not get through all twelve of your photographs. Some people only get through half that many their first time—they never would have guessed they'd have so much to say. But undoubtedly, there will be some of you who tell a short story about each one of your photos and manage to get through all twelve in half an hour. That's okay too—especially this first time. You may find that you have more you want to say the next time you try this.

Celebrating

The end of a Tale-Telling session seems to cry out for some kind of celebration—a wine toast, the sharing of cake and coffee, maybe even singing a song together. One family I know spontaneously applauded at the end of their first Tale-Telling session, and then, one at a time, went up and kissed Grandpa. In other families, a spontaneous sharing of feelings followed the stories: A granddaughter said, "This was really great, Grandma"; a grandson said, "It was like traveling in a time machine." Another family decided to link hands in a circle and sing an old Italian folk song after their first session was over, and they have done so every time since. This is one of the joys of reinventing a ritual: You can create any part of it you like in any way that seems to fit your family.

Finally, do not let this day end without setting the date for the next Elder Tale . . . the sooner the better.

Elder Tale II: *Snapshots from Your Adult Years*

For your second adventure in Elder Tale–Tell-
ing, select a dozen photographs from your young-
adult and young middle-age years—from when
you moved out of your parents' home to when
your children moved out of yours—and tell sto-
ries suggested by these photographs.

Some of you may find this too great a spread of years for a single session and will want to divide it in half: say, limit this Elder Tale to the years between moving out of your parents' house and the birth of your first child; and make a separate Elder Tale of the years between the birth of your first child and the year your youngest child moved out of your home.

First Set a Date

Ideally, the date for this second session will have been set at the conclusion of the first. If not, set it now and try to make it no more than two months away. This time, you may feel more comfortable about inviting more members of your extended family to be present.

Choosing Photographs

Use the same criteria for picking photos that you did for the first session. Let your spontaneous emotional re-

sponse to a photo be your guide. Where there is emotion, there is a story.

Again, when you are settling on your final twelve photos, try to select for a variety of stages of your adult life as well as for variety of locales and circumstances, say, some about your courtship and marriage, others about your professional life, etc. At a future session, you may want to devote an entire Tale-Telling to courtships and marriage, and another to your career, but at this point we're only looking for "Snapshot" stories—stories that are slices of your life in all its variety.

This, from a great-grandmother:

This photo was taken right after my wedding ceremony. . . . I had some mixed feelings about getting married. I remember thinking what I really wanted was security, to belong someplace. I didn't know what to expect. Robert didn't want to wear a ring. He was much older than I. I don't remember the ceremony, what was said, but I do remember all the sniffling; everyone cried and cried, absolutely awful. I wanted to hear bells ringing, not crying. . . . All those flower bouquets remind me that I wanted the biggest bouquet, but ended up with the smallest. Robert had ordered flowers from the local shop, but I wanted my bouquet to come from his flower garden. He said he never cut flowers from his garden, it was like killing them. I insisted, and, as you can see, I ended up with the smallest bouquet. It was our first disagreement. I didn't understand him then, but I do now. . . . What made me happiest was throwing all the chocolates to the town children run-

ning after our carriage. Some of the children remember that to this day and that was over sixty years ago.

And this from another elder:

This is my favorite photo. I've carried it all these years in my wallet. The photo says it all—financial success beyond my wildest imagination. I'm sitting in the garden waiting for the furniture to arrive. I had just purchased the estate with the profits from my new import/export company. It was the walled-in garden, almost like a sanctuary in the middle of the city that made me choose it. I had worked my way through university, and now I was pleased with myself that I could afford such a fine house and proper garden. At the time, my sole companion was Jack, a great horned owl. Just about fifteen years later, when Hitler started the Second World War, I lost everything. I carry this photo with me to remind me that no matter what misfortune comes my way, I can always succeed again and always have.

Keep on the lookout for the odd photograph as well as for the typical one. For example, you may have a photo (as I do) of someone you only knew for one week during a vacation long ago, but who made a lasting impression on you. The story of that week and of the fantasies you subsequently had about how your life might have been different had you spent more time with her tell a great deal about who you are and were. Or perhaps it's an out-of-focus photograph of a stranger carrying a cello onto a ferryboat.

Such a photo provided this "Snapshot" story for one elder:

I took this photo before I even met that fellow. I found him intriguing, I guess—carrying that big instrument with him onto the ferry we were both taking into Portland. . . . I got into a conversation with him by the deck rail later. Turned out he was an itinerant musician, played recitals at churches and colleges all around the country accompanied by a local pianist. I didn't ask, but I don't think he was getting rich in this line of work. And he said that some of the pianists he had to play with were just godawful. . . . But I do remember feeling some envy of this fellow, always on the road, him and his cello, like the Lone Ranger and Tonto. . . . I was in my twenties at the time, not yet married but working hard. . . . And I think this fellow got me thinking again that a man should see

a bit of the world before he settled down. . . . Of course, I didn't know then that I'd be called up [for the army] in less than a year.

An odd photo, but one with a resonant story attached to it.

When you select photographs of your children—especially of children who will be present at the Tale-Telling—perhaps you can think of stories that show *ways you experienced them that they were probably unaware of at the time.* I am thinking of the simple but powerful story my mother told all of us after looking at this photograph.

There you are, Robi, running happily toward me on my first visit to the TB sanatorium in Arosa. I had left you there to be cured of your tuberculosis. That's what they did in those

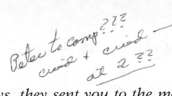

days, they sent you to the mountains for the cure. Well, when I told you I had to leave, you cried and cried, and you didn't stop even after I left. In fact, you made such a fuss that the head of the hospital called me that night in the hotel and instructed me not to return for further visits. He said you became much too upset when I left and would never get better. And stupidly, I followed his advice. I desperately wanted you to get better. You were there for about six months. What you didn't know then was that I would return at night while you were sleeping just to see you, but then I stopped going because that became unbearable for me, to be that close and not be able to hug you. It was the worst period of my whole life, no question about it. Had I known then what I know now, I would have kept right on visiting you. . . . You would have gotten used to my leaving. . . .

I myself didn't remember that incident at all, but I do know that matters of trust and separation have been core themes in my life. As my mother told that story to us, she teared up and so did we. It told us all something remarkable about my mother's love.

Later that evening, Mother's story reminded me how often I had heard elders say, "If only I had known then what I know now," but of course they could not have because the experience of a lifetime was missing.

A word of caution here: It's best to avoid any stories about your children that you think might make them uneasy in front of their spouse or their own children. You may tell your own secrets, but be wary of telling theirs. If there is any question in your mind, simply ask your son or daughter privately if such-and-such a story is okay to tell to the whole family.

Preparation

Again, note down the salient aspects of each of the dozen photos you've selected: the who, what, and where, the special feelings the photo elicited in you, and a reminder of the story or stories associated with it. Put these reminders on a three-by-five card or a Post-it attached to the back of the photo.

You probably will feel less of a need to "rehearse" your performance this time, but if it makes you feel easier to have a practice session under your belt, go ahead and do it.

Telling the Tale

As always, let each story run as long as feels right to you. Don't be eager to go on to the next photo if the one at hand continues to suggest one story after another. Let them roll. You only have to worry about rambling on too long if you find that you are repeating yourself or if you find that you are telling a story by rote, without any genuine emotional connection to it.

Listeners' questions frequently play a greater role in this second session than they did in the first. Some long-repressed "Questions-never-asked" pop up, like, "When did you know you were in love with Mom?" and "How did you feel when Dad said we were going to move away from Milwaukee?"

These questions can lead to more stories, and those stories to more questions. As long as you feel comfortable with this dialogue of questions and stories, let it run, putting the remainder of your photos aside. This dialogue has the potential for producing stories that can directly link one generation to another, so if this means postponing the stories of some of your other photos until next session, so be it.

Still, remember, if any question feels uncomfortable, if you feel that it goes too far—or, perhaps, just too far for now—put it on hold. Say, "Let me try to answer that another time," and move right on to your next photo.

The second Elder's Tale often runs longer than the first—in some cases up to two hours. You may keep going that long if you don't tire and if none of your young listeners are getting tired or fidgety.

Celebrating

As you did the first time, close the session with some kind of ritual celebration, anything from a kiss for Grandma to a toast to a song to a sharing of feelings. And finally, don't let the day end without setting the date for Elder Tale III.

Elder Tale III: *A Day in Your Life*

For your third Elder Tale, try to recall a single day from your youth—from the period when you were still living at home with your parents—and recreate it in stories.

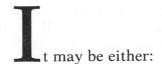

It may be either:

A) An ordinary, routine day—say, a typical school day from when you were nine or ten. Or . . .
B) A holiday—say, Easter or July Fourth as you celebrated it at home long ago. Or . . .
C) A unique day in history as you remember it—say, the day World War I ended or Black Tuesday. Or . . .
D) A unique day in your personal history—say, the day your father joined the army, the day you moved away from the town where you were born, or the day your mother died.

To start with, choose a day from whichever of these categories feels most comfortable for you. Some people feel better able to remember and re-create a *typical* day (or part thereof), while others may feel they have more to work with if it is a *specific* day.

Then, for your next session, you may want to choose a day from a different category to recall and re-create. Some of you may end up telling tales from both categories at the same sitting.

Story Elements

Good storytelling is always in the details. Yes, you had breakfast before you set off for school, but what exactly did you eat for a typical breakfast? How did it smell? How did it taste? Did the whole family eat together? Did your father read the paper at the table? Did your mother serve you? The maid? Did you serve yourself? Was there a neighbor boy who used to stop by to pick you up on his way to school and somehow always ended up having a second breakfast in your kitchen?

Try to recall and describe as many of these details as you can when you tell the story of "A Day in Your Life." The details give your story texture; the details make your remembered experience real for the listener. You may worry that too many details will slow down your story—this is a concern of professional writers too. But in general, Tale-Tellers usually err on the side of too *few* details.

Here's an excerpt from one elder's nicely detailed "typical day" story:

Every night from May to September, the whole family would sit on the front porch after supper. Everybody on our street did it, probably just about everybody in the whole town. My dad would sit on the far side with the Journal *in front of his face and a pitcher of ice tea on a wicker table next to him. Mother and [my two sisters] would usually sew—never mending, you didn't do that in public, for some reason—but they'd be working on a dress or a quilt. My brother read a comic book. And I'd bounce a ball against the steps until my father said it bothered the hell out of him, and then I'd sit in the swing and look over at the Armbrusters next door doing exactly the same things we were. Sometimes I'd think, Why did God make both us and the Armbrusters when He was just duplicating Himself? . . . Later on, when Dad finished the paper, he might say to me, "Let's go down to the [train] station and watch the cops pick up hoboes."*

And here's an excerpt from another:

I remember the blackouts in the Second War. . . . We were poor, dirt poor, like most blacks then—no electricity, no hot water, a toilet bowl in the cellar, dirty floor. No television, no phones; we did have a radio, and we used kerosene lamps. If we had to go anywhere at night in the house, we'd take a candle. . . .

I'm a little boy, six or seven. . . . It's winter, and we get sent to bed at six o'clock—no fooling around. I have four sisters, two of them twins one year younger than I am. We all sleep in the same bed. Not unusual to have three, four people in every bed. . . . Our house is blacked out because we don't want German bombers to come over and see us, which I think is amazingly funny because me and my sisters, we can't figure out why the hell the Germans would want to bomb the dump we live in. . . . But you see, we're still full of energy, but can't make much noise because my mother will come in with the strap. So I tell my sisters stories. These stories go on from night to night. I make them up as I go along. . . . Tonight's story is called "The Red German Revolver," and the hero is a black guy, as always. Of course, in those days, there were no black heroes, but my sisters love it. They have about a thimbleful of courage in the real world, but they were tigers when we used to lay in that bed, trying to keep warm, talking about triumphing over the Nazis and everything else that's bad in the world. . . .

It is natural—but not absolutely necessary—to re-create the "Day in Your Life" in chronological order. For "typical day" stories, this will probably mean telling what happened to you from getting out of bed in the morning to getting back in it at night. For unique days, however, you will more likely begin your story nearer to a dramatic moment in the day.

Here's how one elder began his story of a unique day in his youth:

We were playing touch football in the lot behind the drug-store. The regular game with the regular crowd. . . . And this I remember as if it were yesterday: I went out for a long pass, stretched my arms way out, and when I caught the ball, I had to leap for it, but I still had hold of the ball. Then I heard this burst of cheering, and I thought, Boy, I'm terrific, when suddenly I saw people yelling out their windows. Then I heard it. "The war is over! The war is over!" That's what all the cheering was about. And even though I knew that meant my father would be coming home, my first feeling was, "Hell, I thought they were cheering for me!"

This story then moved on to the young football player running home, then to a church service with his mother and sister, and finally to a fireworks celebration in the park.

The people you encountered during this "Day in Your Life" are the characters of your story. Once again, details are what make these characters come alive. How old were your parents on this particular day? How did they look? How did they dress? (A photograph will help here, although you'll have to fill in the colors.) How did they talk?

Describe all the significant people of this day in as much detail as you can. And try to remember how you reacted to them. Were you wary of your father at the breakfast table? Afraid something you'd say would make him snap at you? Or was he expansive and fun—say, always teasing you about the way your hair looked? Your responses to the people in your day let the listener into your world, allow him to share your re-created experience.

One of the best ways to make your day and the people in it come alive is to try to re-create little *scenes* of that day complete with exchanges of dialogue. Obviously, you can't remember what anyone actually said fifty or sixty years ago. For that matter, you probably won't be able to recall the topics of conversation at breakfast that day. But none of that really matters. What you are trying to re-create is the *feel* of that day, the *sense* of it. What *kind* of exchanges did you usually have at the breakfast table? What *kind* of things did your mother say on the night the Armistice was declared? Dramatize the scene the best you can. Put pieces of dialogue in your parents' mouths that ring true. You are not only *allowed* to take liberties of imagination, you are *encouraged* to. Get creative. The truth of a story is in the feelings it creates. If those feelings are true to the way you remember experiencing that long-ago day, then your story is in a sense perfectly accurate.

Here again is an excerpt from the typical day of the elder whose front porch we visited earlier:

Whenever anybody asked my mother how she was, she'd answer, "If I felt any better, I couldn't stand it."

I don't know how she got started saying that, but she probably said it a dozen or so times every day of her life.

My brother, Carl, who was the funny one in our family, liked to do dumb variations on Mom's expression. . . . Down the stairs he comes this particular morning, and my sister, always the good straight man, asks him how he is.

"If I felt any better, I'd be arrested for indecency,"
Carl says.

"Watch your tongue," my mother says, taking his pancakes off the griddle. She said that a lot too. She had a keen ear for disrespect.

"Don't worry, Mom, I don't really feel that good at all,"
Carl answers her.

And then my mother, all confused as she sets his food in front of him, says, "I'm sorry to hear that, darling."

There is another realm of detail that makes the story of "A Day in Your Life" come alive: sensory details, the sounds, textures, and odors of life. Try to describe the way the air smelled, the way a breeze felt, the sound of the school bell, the taste of fresh homemade ice cream. As you'll see, you'll be able to supply some of these sensory details with props and samples—there's no better way to describe the taste of fresh-made blueberry ice cream than to make some and pass bowls of it around.

Props, Prompters, and Special Effects

Preparation for an "A Day in Your Life" story is more elaborate than for a "Snapshot" story. This Tale-Telling is a production—you are now venturing into the realm of show business.

The props you choose for the telling of this story will probably go far beyond just snapshots. It might be a personal object you still have in your possession from that long-ago day—say, a button from the 1939 World's Fair that says, "I HAVE SEEN THE FUTURE," the model airplane you built with your father, your old teddy bear with a harmonica attached to its paws. Or it may be a public object that relates to that day—say, a newspaper or magazine from that day (or maybe just a news clipping in a scrapbook), a phonograph record of a song that was popular then, a cassette of a radio news broadcast of that day. Or it might be a book you were reading around that time or a lesson you were learning. It could even be a video cassette of a newsreel or a movie that was popular then. And, of course, there are those wonderful eatable props, like the above-mentioned blueberry ice cream.

You can use these props any way you wish—simply as items to pass around at the appropriate moment in the Tale-Telling as you did earlier with your snapshots. Or you may give your props more "production value" by integrating them into your story—say, by using the record of the popular song as background music as you tell your story.

You may want to ask a family member for some help gathering your props. As I mentioned in Chapter 3, the public library is an invaluable source for old newspapers, magazines, and memorabilia albums, as well as, often, for old phonograph records. I also noted there some video catalogs that offer old films and newsreels, as well as catalogs that carry audiotapes of historical radio programs. You'll probably also want to ask a family member or members to assist you in baking, cooking, or ice-cream preparation if you are going to provide some eatable props. (Our family had a ball helping my mother prepare her famous elderflower champagne.) In some families, this "kitchen wisdom" has already been passed from one generation to another, but there will be many of you for which this will be the first opportunity to share a family recipe or technique with a grandchild—and that can be an Elder Tale in itself.

For your first "Day in Your Life," you'll probably want to prepare more extensive notes than you did for your "Snapshot" stories. Maybe a notebook page for each section of the day you'll be describing—say, a page for morning chores, breakfast, and getting to school, another for school, another for what you did after school up to dinner, etc. Put down key words that will prompt scenes and sections of your story—e.g., *Breakfast—Dad grumpy, Eliza chattering, corn fritters, late to school. . . .*

Again, resist trying to write *everything* down. By now, you've probably realized that you have stories to tell, and they don't need to be completely prescripted for you to tell them.

Telling the Tale

We've found it best to begin "A Day in Your Life" stories by laying out the basic facts of the day to be re-created. For example, begin with: "The day is April 18, 1921. I'm twelve years old. My sister, Eliza, is nine, my brother, 'Hap,' is five. My mother is thirty-one, my father thirty-two. We are living in the brownstone where I was born in South Milwaukee. It's Tuesday, a school day, and I wake up wishing it were a Saturday."

Note that the story begins in the present tense, helping to establish the idea of re-creating the day rather than simply describing it. Try to stick to telling your story this way— "I go out in the yard to feed Elmo, our dog, who is waiting for me next to Father's toolshed. . . ."

We've found it best to exclude question-asking during this session—it breaks the flow of the connected stories. If at the end of the session someone has a question related to the stories, she can pose it then.

This session usually runs longer than an hour, but if not, and you feel like it, you may want to go right to telling an "A Day in Your Life" story from another category.

Celebrating

For many reasons (most of which I'm not even sure of), "A Day in Your Life" sessions usually put families into wonderfully happy moods. As the Tale-Telling ends, and everyone returns from this communal time travel, they often want to do something active, like go out for a walk or a ride. A family walk can be a great celebration in itself.

Elder Tale IV: *Turning Points*

In every person's life, there are critical points that, from that moment onward, alter the course of his or her life. Usually, these turning points are precipitated by a crisis. A decision has to be made. You have to declare who you are and what you want in order to move on. And, by action or default, you do move on. Now, looking back, you can see that this was a turning point in your life, that the way you responded to that crisis defined who you are.

Often these turning points involve dilemmas—whether to stay with someone or to leave him, whether to change the way you are living or not to. It may ultimately be your sense of self that is at stake at this critical point—what you stand for, who or what you identify with, what makes your life worth living.

Here's a short section of a Turning-Point Tale one elder told to her family:

I was only sixteen when your grandfather asked me to marry him. It was in a drugstore. He said he had to know one way or the other before they shipped him overseas. He had the ring with him—his mother's, this ring on my finger right here. I can't begin to tell you what went through my head. I wasn't sure I loved him. I didn't even want to love him, not really, not with him going off to war and the chance I'd never see him again. And I wanted more than anything to finish high school. So I told him no. I said, "Joe, I can promise you I won't marry anyone else before you come back, but I can't promise to marry you." I don't know where I got the nerve to say that—I cried every night for a month after I said it. . . .

Of course, I did marry Grandpa as soon as he came back, but I know my waiting and thinking it over and taking that chance gave strength to our marriage. At least, it gave me strength in it.

And here's part of another:

I'd been working in my father's furniture store after school, on weekends and vacations, since I was ten, maybe even younger. By the time I was fourteen, I knew that he expected me to join him in the business as soon as I finished school, and I already knew I didn't want to—that I'd just die in there with all those sofas and lampshades. I didn't even know I wanted to be a teacher then: I just knew, Please God, no furniture store. Well, the dreaded day came when I was seventeen. My father called me into his office on a day near the end of the summer and said he had something to show me. He took out these billing slips that had just come in from the printer, and they had my name printed next to my father's across the top. I'd had years to prepare myself for this moment, and here it was, and I couldn't say anything. I just nodded and said, "Great" or "Thanks" or something false like that. The next morning I took a tram downtown and signed up for four years in the navy. I didn't tell a soul, not even my mother, until the day I left for boot camp. My father didn't speak to me again until I was twenty-five years old and married and living out here in California.

And part of another:

The doctor came out, and he said, "How long have you been drinking, Dominique?" And I said, "I don't drink very much." And he said, "If you want to live to see fifty, you'd better not drink at all." Well, I left that doctor's office and stayed drunk for a week. At the end of that week, I was having visions of angels wagging their fingers at me, and I was so sick I thought I'd die on the spot. I somehow got myself to a phone and called my sister, Lucy, and asked her if she still went to

A.A. Well, Lucy drove all the way up from Kennebunkport that night to take me to my first meeting. Saved my life.

Not all the turning points of our lives are compressed into dramatic either/or scenes like the ones above. Often, you don't even realize that a moment or period was a turning point until long after it has past. Perhaps it was a "road not taken"—a choice you *didn't* make. Here's one of those:

My parents left Palermo for New Jersey when I was twenty-two. My two brothers and three sisters were going with them. Uncle Tonio and Uncle Tulio were already in America. A couple of days I'd wake up thinking, What if I stayed here in Palermo by myself? Kept my boat. Stayed with my friends. But when the day came, I just sold my boat and went with the rest of the family. . . . But I tell you this, in fifty years I am here, not one day I don't wonder how things would have been if I'd stayed in Palermo. I don't say I regret anything. I just wonder.

And part of another:

My father was a mechanic, and I was twelve when I bought my first car, a '31 Model A Ford for twenty-five dollars. . . . I'd tear it apart and rebuild it. I was always making things. . . . Well, here's where I missed the boat: One time when I was only fourteen, I got an old fan blade off one of the cars, a four-bladed one, and I rigged it up to a washing-machine motor my uncle gave me, an old one-cylinder Maytag washing machine. And I put a handle on it and a couple of wheels and used it to cut weeds with. I'd invented the first rotary power lawn mower! But my father was afraid I was going to get hurt, and he made me take it apart. I did, of course. . . . But even at fourteen, I thought, I got something here. I just didn't know what to do with it.

And often it is a decision *not* to do something, to keep the status quo:

My boss, David Korbin, took me out to lunch and told me about the new office the company was opening in Austin. He said if I was willing to relocate, there would be good opportunities for advancement for me. Well, [your mother] and I must have talked about whether to go to Texas every waking hour for a week, and at the end of that week we decided to do it, that it'd be the best thing for my career. Well, the day I was going to tell David our decision, Mother and I had breakfast in the sunroom as usual, and as she was pouring my second cup of coffee, I just looked up at her and said, "If you don't mind, Mary, I think I'd like to stay right here in our house." And she said, "I don't mind at all, John," and that's exactly what we did.

There are also critical junctures when it is not so much a decision that is made as your personality or character that asserts itself. Without thinking, you did what you had to do, and that story tells volumes about the course you've taken throughout your life. Here's one such story that my mother, Emmi, told all of us:

I had prepared for months for my poetry-recital tour of Germany, Hamburg was first. Naturally, I was nervous starting a new tour with all new material. And Germany was in chaos—Hitler had just been given dictatorial powers. I arrived in Hamburg, and the manager received me at the station and he took me to the concert hall. . . . We had dinner with a professor of literature. I remember how enthusiastic they were about my program. I was worried about how my voice would hold up and was wondering whether my old actor friends from Max Reinhardt's would show up. . . . Before I knew it, I was onstage ready to begin, when the theater manager came running onstage. "Don't forget the 'Heil, Hitler,' Frau Akeret, the 'Heil, Hitler.' I was stunned. Speechless. How I wanted to give that recital, but the "Heil, Hitler" was abhorrent. "This I shall never do!" I shouted, and I just walked off the stage. . . . I took the night train back to Switzerland, crying all the way, thinking my career was over. . . . But there was nothing else I could have done.

And there can be turning points in our lives that happen as accidents, some of them fortuitous:

I had to wait for my cousin, Lila, in the library, so I read magazines for a while, and then I just picked up a book that was sitting on the table in front of me and started flipping through it. It was an illustrated book about inlaid wood furnishings in Belgium. I don't believe I'd even heard of Belgium at that point in my young life, but I was transported by what I saw in that book. I'd never put my eyes on anything so beautiful. And so that was that. I was fifteen years old, and I knew right then and there that what I wanted to do with my life was find a way to be near beautiful hand-made objects. . . . Many years later, I tried to find that illustrated book. It was long out of print, but I found it. I'm sure this book is what made me end up in the antiques business.

Pain and Perspective

In every life, there are painful turning points—a marriage or love affair that ends, a friendship that is betrayed, a job that is lost, an illness or handicap that takes its toll— and from that point on, nothing in life is ever quite the same again. Yet looking back from the perspective of age, an elder can often see how these painful turning points were a natural part of his life's development, that they provided opportunities for him to change and grow and to define himself in new ways.

I wouldn't presume to suggest that we all should become Pollyannas in our old age, that we should attempt to look back at our pasts through rose-colored glasses that filter out the pain of our losses, betrayals, and failures. But I can say this: As you put together your stories and start to see the entire sweep of your life, you may start to see an inner logic to the way you moved from turning point to turning point. You may see how, in a sense, your crises and their resolutions were necessary for you to become who you are. The eminent psychoanalyst Erik Erikson sees crisis as an essential element of human development. He believes it prepares us to meet new conditions, to experience a richness of living that a life without crisis could never possess.

Here is part of a painful Turning-Point Tale:

The eye doctor talked with my parents first—left me out in the waiting room for what seemed like hours before he called me in. I knew from their faces what he was going to say—that I'd have to wear glasses, which meant I'd never be a ballplayer. There weren't any shatterproof glasses or contact lenses in those days. Well, for seventeen years all I'd ever thought about was being a baseball player—second baseman on the St. Louis Browns to be precise. I started to swear, right there in front of my mother, something I'd never done before. I said they were all full of crap, that I could see well enough a week ago to hit three homers. But the doctor told me my headaches would only get worse if I didn't wear glasses. I knew he was right, but I fought with everybody for days. Then I begged my parents to let me switch high schools because I didn't want to come to Willoughby with glasses after having been their best ballplayer in twenty years. I'll never forget what my father said. He said I wasn't going to switch anything. He said everybody in the world had a handicap of one kind or another, but the best people were the ones who knew how to play to their strengths. . . . That was a good one to learn early in life.

From another:

Peter and I had been business partners for eleven years when I found out he'd been siphoning money out of our retirement fund for five of those years. I wanted to kill him. That's all I could think about for weeks. It wasn't the money, of course. It was that Peter and I had started that business together, dreamed about it together, had eaten a million sandwiches together with our sleeves rolled up, and then Bang! . . . I was crushed. Something inside me died, I think. [Your grandmother] once said that it made me a colder man. Maybe. Maybe you have to be a little cold—at least in business—if you don't want your heart broken. But I'll tell you something else—thirty-

five years later when I read in the Milwaukee Journal *that Peter had died, I started to cry like a baby.*

As you start to identify and prepare your Turning-Point Tales, many of you may begin to experience a sense of self-acceptance that you have never felt so fully before. Yes, you will undoubtedly reexperience some of the pain of those critical junctures in your life, but you will also appreciate what personal changes and new experiences followed directly from them. This perspective offers many elders a sense of inner integrity, a wholeness, which Erikson sees as the hallmark of this culminating stage of human development. This wholeness is, he believes, the basic source of elder wisdom.

That wisdom is what will give these Turning-Point Tales so much power for your listeners. Hearing you tell the stories of your turning points from the vantage point of self-acceptance can provide your children and grandchildren with a taste of transcendence in their own lives. It can allow them to view the crises they are experiencing in the midst of their generative years from the perspective of a *fully-lived life.* And that perspective, from time immemorial, has been part of the wisdom that elders provide for the young.

From the grandson of the elder quoted above:

I never heard the story about Grandpa Aaron's business partner before—the one who stole money from him. But something about hearing it now was incredibly relieving to me. It seemed to finally explain the wariness and skepticism that all the men in our family carry around with us, along with a general contempt for the world of business that I'm always wrestling with myself. But to me, the whole point [of Grandpa's story] was that he hasn't really turned cold after all. Not inside. I mean, he could still cry when the friend who betrayed him died.

Finding the Story That Tells the Story

You may be surprised how quickly and easily you remember your turning points once you've turned your mind in the right direction. A number of these will probably be stories that you've thought about often—and perhaps even told several times before. Subtler stories and stories that were once quite painful may take longer to surface; they may even require a bit of digging.

Again, a photograph may offer clues—especially if you are equipped with the tools of photoanalysis. And look to your dreams, too, of course. As we've seen, the dreams we dream once we've embarked on the Elder Tale adventure often offer clues to the critical points in our lives. And naturally, letters and journals can help us recall our crises and their resolutions.

Usually, the hardest part is not in recalling the critical points in your life, but in remembering the specific personal scenes that illuminate those points. These are, in a way, the same dramatic scenes that every playwright and storyteller looks for. For example, Phillip, the man who had to give up his dreams of playing baseball because of his failing eyesight, was able to recall the perfect scenes to convey his feelings and reactions: The scene of waiting anxiously outside the eye doctor's office and the scene of his father informing him that he couldn't switch schools and why. Very simply, they pinpoint what was powerful and important about this turning point in his life.

As you think back to a critical period in your life, the culminating scene of a crisis will probably come easily— that moment when you made up your mind, when you declared yourself or otherwise responded to your dilemma. More difficult is remembering the most salient scenes *surrounding* that moment. Instead of racking your memory, often the most effective way to uncover these scenes is to reconstruct events almost as if they'd happened to someone else. Ask yourself what logically and naturally would have led up to that culminating scene? When—logically—could you have learned about your dilemma? Who might have been there? Who might you have talked to about it? Memory will follow logic. And as always, your emotions will alert you when you come near to a significant scene.

Phillip was able to reconstruct for me how he remembered that emotionally loaded scene of waiting outside the eye doctor's office:

At first, I couldn't recall whether it was the doctor or my parents who told me I'd have to wear glasses. It seemed logical that a doctor would have told me—otherwise, I doubt I would have ever believed it. Still, I had this feeling that my parents had told me. Then I thought, maybe all three were there. I puzzled about this for a bit, and then suddenly I got this image: me looking at my father's profile though the frosted-glass window of the door to the eye doctor's office. When I remembered that, I felt my skin prickle. . . . and then I remembered it all—waiting outside the office, walking in, that whole awful moment in my life.

The Big Buildup

All of the above excerpts from Turning-Point Tales have been cut and pruned so I could use them as brief examples. But, in fact, the best of them went on at much greater length—especially the buildups.

When you tell your Turning-Point Tale, you'll undoubtedly be tempted to start at the conclusion—that moment of high drama when you made your fateful decision or life-changing discovery. *Resist that temptation.* Good storytelling always means good buildups, not simply so you'll be more entertaining, but so you can best communicate the power and meaning of the event in your life. For example, when Phillip told his giving-up-baseball story, he began by recounting a state high school championship game he played in—a game where a St. Louis Browns scout was rumored to have been spotted. Then he gave a detailed account of what his room at home looked like: the baseball pennants on the walls, the trophies, the team pictures. He piled one story and image onto another until all of his listeners could feel exactly what baseball had meant to him. Then Phillip (who, I have to admit, is a born storyteller) told about being sent home from school with his first eyestrain migraine, and his listeners experienced an awful foreboding. Slowly and deliberately, Phillip built up to the scene outside the eye doctor's office so that his listeners were sitting there with him, feeling what was at stake for him as he waited for the doctor's verdict.

Describe your feelings in as much detail as you can at every point in your story. Recall, if you can, how you saw the alternatives of your dilemma—what options you felt were available to you. Try to remember what influences were at work on you—in whom you confided, whom you tried to please. Try also to remember what fantasies presented themselves to you. For example, Aaron recounted to his family how he fantasized about killing the business partner who had betrayed him:

It started out as just kind of a movie scene that played automatically in my head. I saw myself buying a gun, going over to Peter's house, and shooting him in the heart when he opened the door—never in the head, always in the heart. Right after imagining that, I noticed that I felt tremendously relieved. So from then on, whenever the pressure of my hatred for him got so bad that I couldn't think straight, I'd run that scene through my head again. I never believed for a minute that I'd really shoot Peter, but that gives you an idea of how angry I was.

Epilogues

Your listeners will want to know what happened *after* your turning points too. Looking back now, how would you say these events fit into the whole of your life? How did your critical discovery or choice influence what followed?

How did it change you? The way you thought and felt? Your relationships? Your expectations for the future? The decisions you made afterward?

The answers to questions such as these will give your Turning-Point Tale context. Here, you may feel ready to generalize, to say how this story represents a theme in your life. Phillip, for example, suggested a lifelong theme when he said his father's prescription to "play to your strengths" was a good lesson to learn early in life; obviously, he took that lesson to heart. And Alice, the woman who wouldn't commit to marriage until she had finished high school, stressed the strength that her daring (for those days) independence gave to her; she saw this as critical to her definition of herself.

Often, you will find that you can illuminate your stories by relating your personal themes to themes in books that you've read or films that you've seen. John, the man who decided at the last moment to forsake a better job in order to stay in the home that he loved, compared his decision and the life he led as the result of it to the lives of characters in two of his favorite movies: the father in *Meet Me in St. Louis,* a man who also made a decision to give up a career opportunity to stay in his hometown; and the Jimmy Stewart character in *It's a Wonderful Life,* a man who, with the help of an angel, discovered that his "ordinary" life was ultimately much richer than the adventurous life he had fantasized about.

John told his family:

I was old-fashioned when I was still young—before it was even fashionable. When Judy Garland sings, "Have Yourself a Very Merry Christmas" [sic] in Meet Me in St. Louis, *I can't for the life of me imagine a reason why any man would want to leave the home he loves. If I was ever ashamed of being an ordinary man, I made my peace with that the day I decided to keep on having my coffee in the same sunroom for the rest of my life.*

Preparation

You will probably come up with anywhere from a half-dozen to two dozen Turning-Point Tales. Of these, I think it's best to have five or six ready to tell at a single session, although, chances are, you will get to fewer than that.

It's likely that you will want to jot down more extensive "crib notes" for your Turning-Point Tales than you have for earlier sessions. Some people have found it helpful to list the main scenes of their story in order. For example, Phillip put down:

1. Baseball Championship
2. Coming home with headache
3. Outside Dr.'s office
4. Father's lecture on "strength."

Of course, he knew every one of these scenes inside and out long before he sat down with his family to tell his stories, but he also knew he had a tendency to get ahead of himself when he told stories—to jump to the end before he adequately established the beginning. So he had his little list on a three-by-five card in his lap to remind him not to skip the buildup.

Some of you may want to prepare props for these stories: photographs, journals, letters, newspaper clippings, and other mementos. Phillip put together quite a package for his story, including a faded photograph of his high school championship baseball team cut from a newspaper and, remarkably, his first pair of wire-rimmed glasses. Annie, the woman who became an antiques dealer and collector, brought along the book on Belgian furniture that played such a pivotal role in her life.

Telling the Tale

As always, make the setting casual and comfortable, and be sure the recorder—audio or video—is ready to go.

Even more than before, take your time telling these stories. They are potentially packed with emotion for everyone, so resist rushing through feelings or cutting them short. And remember, details are the soul of your story—images, feelings, a snatch of dialogue you've reconstructed. Details are what allow your listeners to reexperience the scenes of your life with you.

There are usually a number of questions that come up after each Turning-Point Tale is told. A son or daughter may confess with wonder that he or she never knew the story you just told or, at least, how prominently that event had figured in your life. Very likely, each will want to know more about a different aspect of your story. Aaron's son, for example, wanted to know what it felt like going to work every day during the period that Aaron was dissolving his partnership with his betraying friend, while his grandson wanted to know if Aaron had ever considered getting out of business altogether and going into a different kind of work. And often, listeners' questions ineluctably lead into stories of their own, stories of their own parallel experiences, stories that show family themes that cross generations. Aaron's grandson (a photographer) told the story of a magazine editor who had cheated him and how his wife told him he took it much too personally.

"I'm just a softy, like you, Aaron," he said at the Elder Tale session.

Celebrating

A toast, a song, a walk. Celebrate in any way you want. But be forewarned: Celebrations following Turning-Point Tales have a tendency to turn into love-ins.

Elder Tale V: *High Points and Low Points*

W̲e all have them: victories and failures, achievements and disappointments, great joys and great sorrows. Though you may have covered many of these high and low points in your Turning-Point Tales, there may be others that you didn't see so much as turning points, but rather as the peaks and valleys of your life. These events, too, delineate your personal landscape.

High Points

Most High-Point Tales are relatively easy to recognize and remember: the home runs and promotions, hearts won and duels triumphant, honors and celebrations. Although at this stage of your life some of these high points may not seem as earthshaking as they did when they happened, these stories remain important to tell. For one thing, they portray your dreams, and your dreams, when the last tales are told, often tell more about you than your actual accomplishments.

Usually, elders take this opportunity to talk about high points in their careers, in their marriages, and in raising their families: the cases won, the promotions and raises, the proposals and wedding days, the births of children. And sometimes they tell of fortuitous thrilling moments in their lives. Here is one told to her children by a nurse-midwife:

I remember, after working in Appalachia, coming to New York for training as a midwife. Then I stayed on finding work in my new specialty. I loved working with pregnant women, helping families have a good beginning, but I lacked confi-

dence as a new midwife. My supervisor didn't help. She had a way of pointing out every little mistake, and she couldn't bring herself to say anything positive.

I also lacked sophistication in the ways of the city because I had only lived and worked in very rural settings. I dressed differently, more plainly. And the pregnant women wore make-up and jewelry as did most of the other nurses. I remember one of the nurses who gave me a particular hard time. She asked me once if everyone in Vermont, where she knew I was from, was as plain as I. That hurt a lot. I wanted to run, quit my job. But I loved the work with the pregnant women, helping families have a good beginning. It didn't take too long to get over the shyness in getting to know these pregnant women, but it was hard to let go afterward.

I remember Mildred especially. She had a long, difficult labor, and I stayed with her throughout. She told me of the births of her other children, how isolated and alone she had felt with no one there to support her. And she told me several times how glad she was I was with her. Finally she gave birth to a healthy boy.

Later when I entered the postpartum area, Mildred announced, "There she is." All the other women turned their heads and stared at me with beaming smiles. . . . Several said Mildred was lucky to have had me. Well I can tell you I felt just like a queen.

"Small" High-Point Tales are often the most powerful. Here's one I happen to like especially:

In basic [training], I bunked next to this guy from Toledo named Alfred. A bigger bastard I never met before or since. Alfred set out to make my life miserable from the get-go, and he managed very well for six straight weeks—getting me on report almost every day, putting a dead fish in my canteen, almost getting me killed once on a bivouac. . . . Now there was one thing I could do better than any man down there, and that was to take apart and put together a rifle with the clock on me. I had a natural talent for it. Well, somebody got a bet started that I could beat any man in the barracks doing it—

with me blindfolded. Alfred challenged me. Put up a full week's pay on it. . . . Comes the day of the contest, the sarge is there, and just as we're about to start, he says, "Okay, switch weapons." Alfred refused, said he was more familiar with his own weapon. The sarge said all weapons are the same, and wouldn't let him back out of it. Turned out, of course, that Alfred had monkeyed with my rifle the night before—filed some thread off a screw. So, not only did I win hands down, but Alfred got paid back in spades—forty-eight hours on latrine duty for damaging army issue. . . . I don't think I ever enjoyed winning something so much in my life, not in the fifty-five years since.

Grandchildren, especially, respond to stories of the minor triumphs of your youth—the day you turned the tables on a bully or on a mean teacher, the swimming race you secretly trained for and won, the day you finally captured the heart of the boy who sat in front of you in American history.

Here's a High-Point Tale told by an elder that focuses not on her own achievements, but on the achievements of her remarkable father:

We lived in a small university town. My father was professor of physics. About explaining things, he would say, "If you can't explain it to anybody else, you haven't understood it in the first place." . . . I remember in school we had a kind of stupid chemistry teacher: he would explain a phenomenon, and we in the class usually didn't understand it. But he knew I would go home and ask Father, so the next day he would call on me, and I would repeat the explanations. . . . Now, the day of the Nobel Prize, I had never even thought about this, but my older sister must have had an inkling—she came to school an hour late. She was there when my father received a telephone call from his father, who lived in Berlin, and he had read about it in the Berlin paper before my father was notified. . . . When [my sister] came to school, she met me in the hall and said, "Well, he got it, he got the Nobel Prize." And I said, "Oh, really!"

The students decided to stage a torch parade. I have never seen my father more nervous. He ran up and down the tower of our house to see how the torch parade was progressing. There was a big band playing. Then my father addressed the students, mentioning the nice relationship between the faculty and the students. The students gave Father a resounding, "Hip, Hip, Hurrah!" . . . I was fifteen then, and cannot to this day understand why Father didn't take us along to the ceremony in Sweden. . . . We always tried to have him write about his life— he had lots of things to tell—but he never did.

Low Points

Disappointment, failure, heartbreak . . . no one can live a full life without his share of painful experiences. We often want to forget our low points, but they, too, provide stories that tell who we are. Low-Point Tales may describe a setback in career or finances, a crisis in health, the breakdown of a friendship or marriage, or the death of a loved one. They may tell about a world, national, or community crisis—a war, the Depression, the closing down of a local mill— that took its toll on you and the people around you. Or these tales may describe a period of personal despondency or weakness.

If you are able to tell these stories without overwhelming embarrassment, shame, or pain, you can pass a special quality of wisdom on to your younger listeners. This is because an essential element of any Low-Point Tale is its aftermath: a description of how you weathered your disappointments, how you survived your defeats, how you rebuilt your life after losses. Again, I am not suggesting that your stories should be artificially "upbeat" or inspiring, that you should constantly be on the lookout for the silver lining in every story of defeat or despair. On the contrary, your recollection of your low points should be accurate and uncompromising. But the truth for most of you at this stage of your lives is that you now possess the capacity to view your low points as part of the total sweep of your life. You can see, for example, that pain that seemed at one time as if it would endure forever did finally recede as other parts of your life grew in strength. And you can see what hopes and values gave you the strength to outlive the pain.

One elder told this story to his family:

I'd been selling the Arrow line in what we called the "Golden Triangle"—Hartford, Springfield, and Providence—for eighteen years when they let me go. No warning. Nothing. Just one day I'm the rep, the next day, Good-bye and good luck. . . . I didn't tell anybody for weeks, not Leda, not you children. I just kept going out in the mornings and coming home late at night or sometimes not coming home at all. . . . And I let myself go, drank too much. More than once I thought of stepping in front of a locomotive. . . . I never felt such a failure in my entire life. . . . Later on, after I couldn't keep it a secret anymore, I stayed inside, sat behind the shades in the living room. . . . It was almost six months before I finally got out of that chair and found myself a retail job over at Fox Brothers. . . . Thinking about it now, I realize it was you children that got me out of that chair. I can still see the worry in your eyes as if it was yesterday. And the shame. Thank God for those looks of shame—That's right, if I'd been a man without children, I'm not sure I would have ever gotten out of that chair.

The telling of this story had a profound effect on this elder's family. One grandson, in particular, was deeply moved by it. Later he said to me, "That was the first time I'd heard any man in this family talk about what he owed to his children."

And the elder told me this:

I didn't really know if my boys remembered that period in my life. They were only eight and eleven at the time, and the whole thing only lasted six months—a blink of the eye. My impulse was to leave [the memory] rest. But then I thought, If I'm telling the story of my life, I might as well tell the whole story, right? Well, I saw how they took it when I told it, and now I'm glad I did.

Here is another Low-Point Tale:

This goes back many years, having grown up on a farm, owning my own, still working with my father, having a wife and children of your own. You're looking at a lot of genera- tions. . . . About a dozen of us started farming at the same time, young turkeys, all in our twenties and thirties, all basi- cally good farmers, believed everything the banks and Cornell, all the experts, told us. Get big, buy this, do that. . . . We'll lend you the money—money was cheap, money was free. Go for it, and we all did, and all of a sudden, about 1983, the door slammed shut. We got a letter from our main creditor, the Fed- eral Land Bank, and they said, You can't borrow anymore, and you got to start paying back at a faster rate. Everything was going up, but milk prices were going down.

That's when we got the letter from the government about the dairy termination program, the whole-herd buy-out that Congress had enacted. That letter sealed our fate. . . . I was physically and emotionally burned out. The projections were horrible. If we didn't participate in this buy-out program, we'd have lost the farm. . . . I had to prove that every one of those animals was dead before I got a dime, a piece of paper from the slaughterhouse. . . . It's hard to come home and tell your daughter that you killed her favorite Jersey cow. It's a hard thing.

And here are the opening lines of a Low-Point Tale that moved a family so deeply that they had to stop right there for that day:

On a morning in June exactly seventeen years ago, I woke up at five as I always have done, and before getting out of bed, I leaned down to kiss your grandmother. Her cheek was cold and dry. Something was wrong, and I knew immediately what it was: My Bessie was gone. She'd been taken from me in her sleep.

Context

Just as with Turning-Point Tales, be sure to give both your High-Point and Low-Point Tales context—the circumstances and your feelings that led up to that significant point and the circumstances and feelings that followed it.

But there is another context I want to stress here: In every High-Point and Low-Point Tale-Telling session, be sure to tell stories from both categories. You might try to alternate High-Point and Low-Point Tales throughout the session, although as the above story illustrates, sometimes a family just has to stop after a Low-Point Tale—stop to simply digest and feel and be together. But if you are able to tell stories from both extremes in a single session, you can communicate the range and richness of your life experience. Like the hero of a drama, you can show how you've been up and you've been down, but, yes indeed, you're still here. Again, this context, that a full life has both high points and low points, conveys a quality of wisdom that is unique to elders. Younger family members, caught up in the stresses and conflicts of their own lives, usually find it impossible to see that every fully lived life has its range of ups and downs, triumphs and failures. It has traditionally been the role of the elder to offer this perspective to the younger members of their family or tribe. So it is that in High-Point Tales, you are given complete permission to show off, to tell your achievements with pride, just as you will report your low points with utter candor and honest feeling.

Preparation, Telling, and Celebrating

In preparing your High-Point and Low-Point Tales, observe the same guidelines for developing the scenes of your stories, for preparing yourself with cue cards and props, for pacing your storytelling, for celebrating as in Turning-Point Tales.

Elder Tale VI: *Epiphanies and Lessons*

———————

An epiphany is a sudden realization of a significant truth, usually arising out of a commonplace event. At that special moment, a life meaning becomes clear to you—an insight into your personality, a discovery of something you value or believe in, an acute sense of where you are in life. Such moments are turning points, too, but they are subtle and internal rather than provoked by dramatic events outside you. And yet such moments can determine the course of your life as much as your response to a crisis.

Here's an Epiphany Tale one elder told to her family:

I must have been around seven or eight. It was summer, and we were visiting my aunt Clara up at Crystal Lake. I was alone, lying on my back by the banks of the lake, looking up at the sky, and I had my harmonica in my mouth. I was just breathing through it, in and out, not playing a melody, simply breathing. And suddenly, I was overcome with this wonderful feeling of connection to everything in the world. I'd say now it was a spiritual feeling. I listened to the sound my breathing made through that harmonica, and I thought, I am part of the noise of the world. I am part of everything. . . . I've had that feeling again, from time to time, throughout my life—a certainty that I am part of the universe—but that was my first time. I think that knowledge is one reason I've never found the idea of dying very frightening.

And here's another:

I was on a flight from someplace to someplace else—I can't remember either place anymore. I spent half my life on planes in those days. I was in my mid-forties and vice president of marketing. Anyhow, I was leafing through a magazine when I came across this poem which I have right here. Still carry it in my wallet to this day. Well, when I read it on that plane, I started to cry for the first time since I was a boy. Right there in business class next to a perfect stranger! Reading that poem, I was filled with love for [your mother]. I realized then, as I guess I'd never quite realized before, that her love sustains me in mysterious ways.

At such moments, the truth strikes, and somehow you know it will stay with you. These moments, too, translate into stories that tell who you are. Obviously, they won't have the buildup or length of a Turning-Point or High-Point/Low-Point Tale, yet they may have just as great an impact on your listener.

Here's another Epiphany Tale:

It was a very bad period for me. Both of my parents had died inside of that one year. [Your father] had been passed over for a promotion again—because of the number of consonants in his last name, we thought, although that thought didn't make it any easier. I was angry at everybody—everybody with good jobs and money and parents who were still alive. The world was an ugly place. . . . Well, here's what happened this particular summer night. . . . I couldn't sleep, so I went into the kitchen and turned on the radio and out came this wonderful, sweet music—French ballet music, they said it was later. I just stood there in the kitchen letting that lovely music wash over me, letting it wash me clean. And I said to myself, By God, there are beautiful things in the world, too, not just ugly things. I made a promise to myself to keep an eye out for the beautiful things and listen for them whenever I could. I can't say I've always kept that promise, but I can say that thought has stayed with me at times when I've needed it.

And this Epiphany Tale catches a magical moment of self-discovery.

I was coming home one night from New York and dinner with—who else?—Sallie. I was on this very brightly lit bus, and it was winter, and the seats were packed with businessmen all bundled up with their briefcases in their laps reading the papers or staring ahead. Suddenly tears began streaming down my face. I couldn't stop them. I wasn't unhappy or sad, or particularly happy. I stared straight ahead, just like all the businessmen, as the tears soaked my collar and the knot of my tie, and I imagined myself watching myself from across the aisle, and asking, Why is that person, who is me, staring ahead and crying? The marvel of the moment rested in realizing the full power of the flood of emotions that ever washes around in our brains, ready to spill out. The joy was in being powerless to prevent it, or to try to, or even to care to. I just felt wonderful.

Epiphanies, insights, moments of self-discovery . . . these are the stories that can tell the values we develop over the course of a lifetime, the lessons we live by and, often, the lessons we would like to pass along to the generations that follow us.

Dream Your Way to Epiphanies

Most of your epiphanies will stay with you, but some may be forgotten. In my experience, Epiphany Tales cannot be dug out of memory the way other stories can. Photographs don't usually offer clues to such memories. And although an intimate diary might contain an entry about an epiphany or personal lesson, as might a recovered piece of personal correspondence, by far one of the best methods for retrieving memories of epiphanies are dreams and dream associations. As we saw in Chapter 6, the dreams we dream as we immerse ourselves in life review are frequently rich in material that can lead quite naturally to memories of epiphanies past.

Here one elder reconstructs how a *lebenslauf* dream brought a long forgotten epiphany back to him.

I'd been spending a few days working on Turning-Point stories to tell my family when I had this dream in which I was riding in a subway, and every time I tried to get off, the door slammed closed in my face. I kept growing more and more frustrated until this old black man sitting across from me caught my attention and pointed out the window. Well, we weren't underground after all, we were out in the country, and it was a fine-looking day. Suddenly, I felt quite content. I sat back and enjoyed the scenery. . . .

Next morning, I was jotting this dream down when I abruptly remembered the time I went to my aunt Florence's funeral. I was only thirty-two or -three and hadn't been particularly close to my aunt, but I knew how much my mother would miss her. It was a beautiful fall day, the trees full of color in the graveyard. Well, thinking about this dream, I remembered that I had had an epiphany of sorts standing there by Aunt Florence's graveside. It was an intimation of my own mortality. I'd realized with a shock that I had reached the age when I could no longer think of life stretching endlessly in front of me. And I realized that I had to make the most of things while I could. . . . Not a particularly original thought, I guess, but it felt important, and still does. My dream was about the same thing: I've had a tendency my whole life to feel trapped by things, but when I've just sat back and breathed deep, I've been my happiest.

Telling the Tale

Epiphany and Lesson Tales tend to be short, so you may want to tell them as part of your Turning-Point Tales session. Yet, while these stories themselves are short, they sometimes offer an opportunity for you to talk in general about lessons you've learned that you'd like to pass on. Not sermons—heaven knows, sermons don't "play" well at family gatherings—but simple statements of some of the philosophical ideas that have guided your life and that might prove useful to the rest of your family. It's a chance to sneak in a little wisdom.

In some families, a regular "Seminar on Life" follows in the question-and-answer period. One Epiphany Tale begets another from another family member, then another, and pretty soon everyone is airing his thoughts about some very basic life questions: How do you live with frustrated dreams? Why are some of the most wonderful parts of life the easiest to ignore? Why do we sometimes feel our most intense love for someone when we are furthest away from them? What counts as a "spiritual" experience?

And hundreds more.

If you are videotaping this session, be sure to record the "seminar" too. You'll be surprised how much your family will enjoy viewing this part years from now.

Ⅰn Part II, you began thinking about the themes of your life, how to recognize them and where to find them. By analyzing personal photographs and *lebenslauf* dreams, and by exploring life-story themes in fiction, film, and memoir, you probably started to identify the recurring motifs and "melodies" of your life. In this session, you tell stories based on these themes.

Entitling Yourself

A productive and entertaining way to get this process going is by making a list of working titles for your "memoirs." Try to come up with titles that capture something essential about who you are and the way you've lived. Among my favorite autobiography titles is the war photographer Robert Capa's *Slightly Out of Focus*. That title not only refers to certain specific incidents in Capa's life—like when the D-Day photographs he took at great personal risk were fouled up by a nervous lab technician—but it also refers to the random, unfocused quality of the way Capa lived, a quality that made his life both ultra-exciting and painfully fragmented. Another autobiography title that captures its author to a *T* is Oscar Levant's *Memoirs of an Amnesiac*. The witty pianist's book is filled with the neurotic quirks that ruled his life, both in comic ways—like how, if Levant got out of bed on the "wrong side," he'd compulsively have to get back in and start all over again—and in tragic ways— like how, when his good friend George Gershwin died, he could not get himself to perform in public for years to come. Levant's title evokes a life filled with contradiction, a life bounded by the quirks of a febrile, comic, and neurotic mind. Sammy Davis, Jr.'s, *Yes, I Can*, suggests his lifelong theme of confronting challenges and overcoming odds. Alfred Kazin's, *A Walker in the City*, conveys the image of a moving observer, a sensor of the passing scene, which is exactly the kind of man Kazin is revealed to be in his book.

Free-associate titles for your own memoir. Think of words or phrases that seem to say, "That's the story of my life!" Do any familiar expressions describe overall themes of your life? I'm thinking of simple expressions like "Making Do," and subtler expressions like "Living Well Is the Best Revenge." How about song titles or lines from song lyrics like "With Me, It's All or Nothing," or "I'm Forever Chasing Rainbows"? Are there lines from favorite poems that seem to capture an essential theme of your life? Or is there a nickname you were called at one point of your life that describes something special about you? (A once frenetic and hard-driven elder who had been known at work as "Speedy Gonzales" came up with the witty memoir title "Speedy Slows Down.")

Jot down every little title that pops into your head, whether or not you are absolutely sure it is appropriate. Often a title comes first, and its sense or relevance follows later. Let your list grow over the course of several days. Whenever a title comes to mind with a story or set of stories attached to it, jot them down too.

Stories with Range

Once you have assembled a list of a half-dozen to a dozen working titles, start thinking in earnest of the stories that support these titles. Give as much range to these stories as you can. Try to link stories from your childhood, your young adulthood, and your middle age that all fit under the same rubric.

An elder named Paul came up with the title "Just Kidding, Folks" to describe how, throughout his life, he would pull stunts and tell jokes to get out of tight situations: His first story in this series came from an incident in second grade when a comic impression of Calvin Coolidge saved him from staying after school; his next story was from his army days, when a Ben Blue routine got him out of KP duty. But the story Paul told next in his "Just Kidding, Folks" series provided a surprising and moving moment for his listeners:

When I was nineteen, my grandmother Limm died, and I came back from Missouri for the funeral. I'd been close to Gran Limm, closer than any of the other kids. We could really talk, you see. Well, at the cemetery service, the minister asked people to say a few last words to Grandma—sort of a send-off. My mother went first, then her sisters and brothers, lots of crying, and then I volunteered. And I started telling a joke—Gran Limm loved jokes. God knows what this one was about, probably a traveling salesman, but very quickly everybody was trying to shut me up. But I kept on going. And when I finished, I started laughing like crazy and couldn't stop. . . . I was sick with embarrassment afterward. But you see, joking and laughing was the only way I could bear what I was feeling at that moment. I don't think anybody but my dead grandmother could have appreciated that.

Paul had told more than a simple and amusing anecdote; he had revealed how humor permitted him to survive.

There was, in fact, one elder I know who chose the old song title "I'm Forever Chasing Rainbows" to describe a significant theme in her life. She saw herself as a relentlessly optimistic dreamer, and had stories covering seventy years to prove it—from the time she mailed mash notes to a secret love in the hollow of a tree to the time she took a yearlong correspondence course in starting your own nursery, only to discover that she didn't have sufficient funds to cover her start-up costs.

"Typical me," she told her listeners. "But I always liked the chasing better than the rainbows anyhow."

Another elder chose the title "The Almost-But-Not-Quite Girl" to describe what she saw as the recurring theme of near-misses of personal recognition and success in her life. Her first story was about coming in second in a school talent contest; her last about someone who had beat her to the punch with a business idea in her forties.

Here's an elder who conveyed something about who he was and still is with a ramble of stories under the title: "I'd Be Lost Without Horses, I'd Go Nuts."

I think we lived a lot better back then than today. You didn't have television to goof up your eyes. We had games we'd play. Anthony and Over. Butter/Butter, Fox and Geese in the Snow. Summers we'd ride the horses over to the Moarhouse Bridge, go swimming, take the horses right in the river. They loved that, and we did too. Then we'd draw water in fifty-five-gallon drums. We'd back the wagons right in the river. Couldn't afford to drill a well.

We did more traveling to see our relatives those days with the horses than we do now with the cars. Oh yah, we'd hitch up the sleigh or the wagon, we'd see Gramp. And he'd tell us these stories. I remember one about a fellow asleep on his wagon as it went along. Gramp stopped the team, unhooked the horses—can't believe this, but he said it was true. He turned them around, heading toward the guy driving them, and then Gramp got back to his own team and hollered at the guy. He woke up with his horses looking right at him.

My dad loved horses. He had a milk route, and he peddled for thirteen years, ten cents a quart. Horses pulled the milk wagon. It's the only power we had. In the winter, we always got the wood with them, and the ice. My father would cut ice in the river for two weeks, and in the summer he'd sell it to the farmers, cent and a half a cake. We'd cover the ice with old, wet sawdust. In the spring and fall, we'd take the teams, one man plowing and the other harrowing. And we used to mow hay with them ten years after tractors came in.

I bought my first horse for fifty dollars when I was thirteen. That was a lot of money then, making fifty cents a day. I sent away to Sears & Roebuck—bought a harness for twenty-one dollars on time payment. Paid them three dollars a month.

*My dad and I made a cart for her, and I'd drive her all over.
She was quite a little chestnut.*

*Now I still love to drive horses. We go to these fairs. There's
no money in it, in fact it costs money, but I enjoy it, win or
lose. Then I give the school groups hayrides and sleigh rides—
kindergarten, Head Start, summer camps, anniversaries and
weddings.*

*If I had to do it over, farming, I'd be smaller. I wouldn't
get big. And I'd do it all with horses, I wouldn't even own a
tractor, not even for plowing. They can be a pain, my horses,
taking care of them night and morning, but I'd be lost without
them, I'd go nuts.*

Now it is time to winnow down your list to the three
or four titles with the most revealing and significant stories
attached to them. A single title may have only a pair of
stories subsumed under it, or it may have five or six. Put
the titles and "crib notes" for the stories on three-by-five
cards and decide how many themes you'd like to cover in
your first "That's the Story of My Life" session. Many families end up having several of these sessions on separate occasions.

When you sit down to tell these stories, start with your
title for the story set. If you think the title needs to be ex-
plained, do so, but try not to overexplain. Let your listeners
find the connections between the stories on their own.

The Seminar Continues

The stories you tell in this session are core stories—stories that get to the essence of who you are and how you've
lived. Most will probably not be as highly dramatic as the
stories you told in Turning-Point or High-Point and Low-
Point Tales. That's perfectly okay. In some ways, these stories will tell more about you than the others, particularly
in how much they reveal about how you interpret your own
life. In the examples above, the woman who titled her stories "The Almost-But-Not-Quite Girl" could have called the

same stories "I'm Forever Chasing Rainbows" (and vice versa) and put an entirely different personal spin on her life experiences.

It is because of this extra dimension of self-interpretation that listeners' responses to these stories often generate exciting family discussions. Children and grandchildren often chime in with, "Hey, that's the story of *my* life too!" and add stories of their own. (The granddaughter of the woman who was "forever chasing rainbows" declared, "So that's where I get that from!") And very soon everyone is thinking of titles for her own memoirs.

As before, be sure to record the "seminar" too. And after you've celebrated the end of the session, set your date for the next.

Elder Tale VIII: *Telegrams and Epitaphs*

A s in "That's the Story of My Life," this session provides innovative techniques for digging out and presenting the core stories of your life.

"Telegrams and Epitaphs" is about unique messages: The messages you wish you had conveyed (or could convey) to someone important in your life—and the messages about yourself that you'd like to leave behind for the people who come after you.

Both kinds of messages establish major themes in your life—themes about your relationships to others and themes about how you interpret your life. And both messages can tap into rich lodes of near-forgotten stories.

Telegrams

Compose brief telegrams to those people—living or dead— who have touched your life in a significant way. Have your message tell them something that you wish you'd said before. Think of the stories that explain the meaning of your telegrams.

The telegram can be simple, yet tell a great deal about your feelings. Here's one that one elder in her eighties fired off to her long-departed mother:

Thank you for feeding me when there was no food.

The story that followed that simple ten-word message was indeed a poignant one. Here's part of it:

I was a married woman with children of my own before anybody told me the real story about what our family went through in the winter of '07. . . . My father had gone south to look for work, and my mother was left alone with just the three of us. We had no money and no food. The best my sister could remember—Mother was already gone by then—was that Mother bartered her possessions for food. . . . Her combs, her jewelry, her clothing . . . Well, that was seventy years ago, but I never properly thanked her for that.

And here's a telegram written by another elder:

Brothers . . . I quit! I wish I'd said that sixty years ago.

The story that followed that fiery telegram was poignant in quite a different way:

The brothers this telegram is addressed to are my fraternity brothers at Penn. . . . The second year I was in the house, we had a new president and council, and they decided to put the incoming sophomores through a hazing the likes of which I'd never even imagined. Made those poor bastards guzzle a keg of beer and then march around the quad half-naked for hours on end on one hell of a cold night. . . . One of the boys broke down, cried like a baby, and they threw him out on the spot. . . . Broke the boy's heart. . . . It was wrong, all of it, and I had no business staying in that frat house after that. . . . But I was nineteen and weak, and I never said a word. . . . I'm saying it now.

This remarkable story, filled with power and regret, led to the telling of several other stories that traced a painful theme in this elder's life: stories of times in which he felt he'd been too timid to stand up and be counted. And yet, as his son reminded him later in this session, he was the same man who, in middle age, had quit the local golf club because of its discriminatory policy.

"I had no choice that time," the elder protested, but then finally proudly admitted that perhaps the frat-house incident in his teens—and several other ensuing incidents like it—had prepared him for a show of strength later on in life.

Minor Characters, Major Influences

At this point in the Elder Tale Program, you've undoubtedly told many stories about the major characters in your life: your parents and siblings, your primary friends and business associates, your spouses and children. Now is a good opportunity to think of the minor characters in your life—the people whose lives touched yours briefly, but meaningfully. Think of someone who was a guide or mentor at a critical point in your life—a teacher who gave you confidence when you sorely needed it, that friend you made at a family resort some sixty summers ago who taught you how to dive. Think of someone who had a profound emotional impact on you—your partner in a short-lived romance, the woman sitting across from you on your train journey to California who, over the course of two days, related to you why she was leaving her husband and children. Minor characters who had a powerful impact on you.

Write them telegrams too.

Here's a telegram to a "minor character" one elder wrote:

Miss Spence: Thank you for my library card. It changed my life. Please forgive me for my stupidity.

The story that followed, about how at the age of twelve she was introduced to the world of literature by the local librarian, had a painful ending to it. For two years, this librarian guided her reading, gradually expanding her horizons to include worlds she'd never dreamed of. But then something happened:

A girlfriend from school informed me that Miss Spence lived with another woman and that she was a lesbian. (That's not the word she used, of course.) I was horrified. And I felt like Miss Spence had lied to me or, even worse, been trying to trick me into something terrible. I never returned to that library. In fact, I pretty much stopped reading for the next few years of my life. And one time when I saw Miss Spence walking toward me in the street, I turned my back on her and walked away. I'm sure she knew why. I bet it had happened to her before. How awfully stupid we all were. . . . That was 1922.

And here's a quite different telegram that an eighty-nine-year-old World War I veteran shocked and greatly amused his family with:

To Nicole somewhere on the Rue St. Denis. Thank you for pretending that you didn't know it was the first time for me.

Missing Persons

Remembering the minor characters in your life is not always easy. Often, you don't have personal photographs or correspondence to help bring them to mind. Yearbooks, of course, are frequently a good source, as are copies of old newspapers (especially if you lived in a relatively small town). But most often you will need other techniques to locate these missing persons in your memory.

Time rambling may prove useful here. Pick times and places where you were likely to have had relatively brief put possibly intense encounters with people: a bus, train or plane trip; a summer camp or cottage; a short period of time spent in an unaccustomed city or town for school or business; a college dorm; an army barracks. Try to imagine yourself in that time and place, gradually narrowing the scope of the venue—for example, go from your town to your school to your classroom to your desk and chair in that classroom. As you immerse yourself in this imagining, minor characters from your past are likely to pop up: You remember a face, a routine, a shared joke or intimacy, a special encounter. Feelings follow, and as you identify those feelings, stories and undelivered messages follow too.

Another technique that has proved surprisingly effective for locating minor characters who had a major impact on your life is working backward from telegram messages. Start, for example, with THANK YOU FOR THE ENCOURAGEMENT WHEN I NEEDED IT and then gently ramble through different periods of your life for the appropriate recipient of your message.

Or start with:

YOU SHOCKED ME!

WAS IT MY FAULT?

YOU BROKE MY HEART.

Or: THE WORLD WAS NEVER THE SAME AFTER THAT DAY.

In the mind's tricky way of retrieving lost memories, a quite specific message may pop into your mind before it is attached to a person, time, or place.

For example, one elder told me she was gently rambling through the summers she spent in the family cottage on Cape Cod when this message popped into her mind: WHY DIDN'T YOU EVER WRITE? She continued:

And at that same moment, I got this kind of bittersweet feeling. And then I remembered it all. A girl named Cynthia whose family had rented the cottage next to ours one summer. We made immediate friends and had long, intimate conversations sitting underneath the porch together. At the end of the summer, we were both quite sad and pledged to write each other constantly. . . . I wrote her twice, and both letters came back unopened. They had moved, I think. I never heard from Cynthia again. I think that was the first time anyone had broken my heart.

Telegrams and Tales

In preparation for the Tale-Telling, write your telegrams down exactly as you want to read them. (Some elders created some very real-looking black-type-on-yellow telegrams for the session.) Put your story "crib notes" on an attached sheet or card.

These Elder Tales have a built-in drama that you should exploit for all it is worth: the mystery of your telegram message. What does it mean? What happened in the past to provoke it? To whom is it addressed?

Read your telegram *first*, let your listeners puzzle for a moment, and *then* tell the story that explains your message. Often, related stories about the same person or on the same theme follow naturally. Whether or not you have prepared these stories, let them roll.

Do-It-Yourself Epitaphs

Compose several brief epitaphs for yourself—the headlines you'd like to see on your headstones. Think of them as messages to future generations that convey how you want to be remembered. Now think of the life stories that explain why these epitaphs are appropriate.

These epitaphs and their attendant stories differ from "That's the Story of My Life" stories chiefly in their intent. Yet precisely because you are focusing on how you wish to be remembered, you are likely to come upon themes and stories that have eluded you up to now. This is especially true for elders who always have to wrestle with their modesty when they consider telling a life story. As you consider what messages about yourself you want to pass on to future generations, you automatically put yourself in touch with one of the inherent responsibilities of Elder Tale-Telling: Your stories offer an example—an option for how to live a life— to those who follow. Such has always been the enterprise of elder wisdom, so now is no time for modesty.

Elders I know have come up with a marvelous variety of what we came to call Do-It-Yourself Epitaphs. Here's one:

He Was Happiest When He Was Young, Strongest When He Was Old

The lovely array of stories that followed delivered precisely what that "epitaph" promised: stories of a carefree and irresponsible youth balanced with stories of a late-marrying and hard-working middle and old age.

Here's another:

Family First, Last, and Always

The stories following this one told of family devotion and sacrifice, the basic values this woman hoped would carry on in the generations that came after her. Here is an excerpt from her story:

When you kids were young, your dad and I moved about a great deal, always trying to find better work. First we'd pick the neighborhood with the best public-school system, then we'd look for work. And we always made a point of eating together as a family, not work late. . . . When our marriage started to suffer from all the stresses of the Depression, I worked hard to keep us together, to make it really work—that's all that really mattered to me.

Another:

I'd Rather Be Smelling the Roses (Than Lying Underneath Them)

Written by a life-loving elder with a wry sense of humor, the stories he told to go along with this epitaph described several small moments in his life when he took time out to enjoy nature.

Another:

Wish I Had It All to Do Over Again (So I Could Do It All the Same but Better)

The stories following this epitaph subtly wove the theme of a woman who, although content with the choices she'd made, always felt she had hung back from life.

And another:

He Who Seeks Equality Should Go to a Cemetery.

This elder used this old Yiddish proverb as an ironic comment on his proudly unconventional life.

"Do We Have to Talk About This Now?"

There will be some people who find the very idea of Do-It-Yourself Epitaphs too terribly sad to even consider. Somehow these people invariably turn out to be the younger family members, *not* the elders. On the contrary, most elders find this approach to telling their stories enlivening and quite amusing. In fact, some of the funniest Elder Tales told seem to come out of these sessions.

"It's a great tension-breaker," one elder reported to me. "The next-best thing to being present at your own funeral and telling jokes from the Other Side."

Indeed, most elders and their families tell me these sessions are their most joyous precisely *because* they acknowledge death, rather than continue to deny it.

"We never really talked about death in our family before," one daughter told me. "Only about life insurance and wills and burial plots and who'll get what, but never anything that said straight out, 'I'm going to be gone someday, and here's the way I'd like to be remembered.' It was a relief to all of us, I think. For some reason, it put us all in a very up mood."

A major reason for that "up" mood, I believe, is that in the very act of acknowledging the elder's mortality, everyone acknowledges the *immortality* provided by his Elder Tales.

As one elder put it:

"When you write your own epitaph, you write yourself into your family history. And that's exactly the place where I hope to live on."

All of that said, I must still add that if there are any family members who continue to find the idea of Do-It-Yourself Epitaphs disrespectful or distasteful, skip this particular way of presenting your stories (although you may still find it a useful device for retrieving core stories from your memory).

Telling the Tales

I've purposely placed Telegram Tales and Do-It-Yourself Epitaphs Tales in the same session. Both involve time-traveling messages—to people in your past, from yourself in the future—and somehow they provide a nice balance for one another.

There is no set way to order your stories, but most elders I spoke with felt comfortable doing four or five telegrams and their attendant stories followed by two or three epitaphs and their attendant stories. It makes for one of the liveliest Tale-Telling sessions you'll have.

Again, count on a great deal of response from your listeners—questions, telegrams, and epitaphs of their own. Record it all. This is family history for generations to come.

Elder Tale IX: *Sentimental Journeys*

Travel to a significant landmark of your past. "On location," tell tales that took place there.

This will undoubtedly be the most elaborate (and expensive) session of the program. It will probably also be the most evocative.

By traveling to the actual places where scenes of your life played out, you will at once establish a visual context for your stories—the "scenery" is real—*and* provide yourself with a raft of cues and clues to near-forgotten stories. As we saw in Chapter 3, there is nothing quite like sensory stimulants—the smell of your old grammar school, the sound of the tree frogs at your old camp, the way the light falls through an open window in your old library—to liberate memories that have not risen to consciousness for scores of years.

The Elder Tales you tell on these "Sentimental Journeys" will have a unique power and immediacy for both you and your listeners (and your home viewers who will see the video of your trip). But more than any other step in this program, this one requires careful preparation.

Scouting Locations

The location most elders naturally pick for their initial Sentimental Journey is the first home they remember in the first town or city they lived in. Next comes their school in this town, then the places where they hung out—the drugstore, the café, the ball field, the docks, the library.

Second-highest on most elders' list is a place where a singular dramatic event occurred in their life: the riding camp where my wife and I first met and fell in love some forty-five years ago; the town in the south of France where a young soldier heard the tolling of church bells signaling the end of the war; the hospital where a teenage girl first realized that she wanted a career in medicine.

And the next category from which elders most often pick is the landmarks of their young adult life: the first school or college at which they boarded, the first place where they worked, the first house they bought. The list goes on: the seaside hotel that was once the scene of the happiest vacation of a lifetime; the cemetery where a loved one is buried; the church where First Communion was celebrated.

Picking locations that seem rich in memories is the easy part. "Scouting" which locations are viable becomes more difficult. Personal landmarks, like everything else, have a tendency to change—even to disappear—with the passage of time. Houses are torn down, streets are rerouted, whole neighborhoods become altered beyond recognition. And traveling to a special personal landmark and discovering radical changes can be disheartening. In an essay titled "Writing and Remembering," William Zinsser tells of taking his family out to see the house on Long Island in which he spent his early boyhood, only to discover that the once-rural road on which it sat was now populated with split-level houses and swimming pools, and the house itself was torn apart in the process of being converted to a Beverly Hills–type manse.

To prepare yourself for these changes (and to mitigate against disappointment), some advance research should be done. Often, all it takes to discover the current status of a personal landmark—a house, a school, a store—is a letter of inquiry to the local newspaper, historical society, chamber of commerce, or tourist bureau. (For best results, include a self-addressed, stamped return envelope for the reply.) That failing, a letter of inquiry addressed to "Occupant" of the place in question often yields enlightening replies; in more than one case I know of, such a letter has opened the way to an on-site visit of private premises. If neither of these efforts come through for you, it will probably be necessary to send a "scout" ahead to check out your landmarks—a good job for an enterprising grandchild—before you plan a full-fledged family journey.

Other considerations before you commit yourself to a particular spot are, of course, how far away it is and how expensive it is to get there, and this, in turn, may determine how many family members will be able to come along with you.

In general, I've found it's a good idea to start with a Sentimental Journey that is close to home—only a day trip away, if possible. After that, you'll be ready to plan more distant and extended journeys.

Pack Up Your Emotions in Your Old Kit Bag

Before setting off on a Sentimental Journey, prepare yourself for an emotional adventure. One of the main purposes of this trip is to tap into memories—and *details* of memories—that have been long forgotten. These memories will be reached through your senses: the smell of the wet hay in what was once your grandfather's field suddenly floods you with memories of summer days on his farm; the sound of the tugboat whistle from the bridge by your boyhood apartment brings back memories of crossing this bridge with your old friend, Tom, on the way home from school; the sight of the flag waving outside your old grammar school (now a courthouse) reminds you of the day they marched all you youngsters outside and lowered the flag to half-mast to honor the dead of the *Titanic*. Such sense-induced memories can come fast, and with them often come powerful emotions.

One elder recounted this emotion-packed moment:

I smelled that wet hay, and I found myself remembering exactly what it felt like to sit on top of a haystack and watch my grandfather gather in the hay with a pair of horses drag-

*ging a metal rake behind them. I could practically see them
there in the field. For a moment, it was as if no time had passed
at all, and that is what brought the tears to my eyes. How
close it all seemed. How sweet it all had been. And how quickly
it had all slipped away.*

Another told me of breaking into uncontrollable laughter at the sight of a ten-year-old child with a skateboard
under her arm coming down the steps of her old library.

*Except for the skateboard, that could have been me fifty-
odd years ago. It felt a little like a hallucination must feel—it
made me feel so giddy.*

You can expect to be surprised by your feelings—if that
doesn't sound like a contradiction. You can expect at times
to be overwhelmed by stabs of memory, by a giddy sense
that life is just a dream. But powerful and unexpected as
these sense-evoked memories may be, they are not dangerous. Of the elders I know who have ventured on Sentimental Journeys, most have experienced sudden bursts of
laughter and tears, even fleeting hallucinationlike memory-
fantasies, but none have come away from the experience
depressed or shaken. On the contrary, the thrill of reexper-
iencing moments of the past with such intensity had a remarkably enlivening effect on all the elders I spoke to. And
so I can say with confidence that your best preparation for
this adventure is to try to be open and trusting of your feelings. They are about to take you on the trip of your life.

On the Spot

You've worked out your itinerary, planned which family members will come with you, made sure your camera or
tape-recorder person is properly prepared, bought your
tickets, and taken off for a special landmark of your past.
What do you do when you get there?

First: *Take your time!* Don't rush to tell a story the moment you land on a familiar spot. In fact, most elders prefer to start by venturing alone to the landmark (or with just one other family member) and "soaking it up" for a good long while. Take a slow look around. And while you are at it, take a slow listen around and sniff around too. Drink it all in. Observe the details—the view through the window from what was once your geography classroom, the smell of the old books in the basement of your childhood library, the sound of water lapping against the dock of your old summer camp. . . . Memories come, stories appear.

For the time being, just note them down in brief on a pad or with a memo tape recorder. You don't want to interrupt the flow of your memories by working too hard at recording them. Later on, you can write down more details in preparation for the Tale-Telling.

Sometimes, the stories that come rushing back to you are stories you've already told, except now these stories have more texture and are more loaded with emotion. Tell these stories again when the time comes: I can guarantee you your listeners will be fascinated by hearing them anew with the added details and emotional content.

Undoubtedly, when it comes time to take your family to your personal landmark to tell stories, you'll have several already prepared. Still, leave yourself open to other stories and characters that may come rushing back to you on the spot. Tell these tales too. More than ever, one story will beget another, and that story another as well.

One elder was leading his family on the route he walked from school to home half a century ago, all the while telling them the story of the day he brought home his first failing report card, when abruptly a brown toad jumped out of the tall grass in front of them. The elder's memory suddenly jumped to this new story:

Toads! The things we did with toads! . . . Reggie, a red-haired kid with the devil in him, knew a million ways to cause trouble with toads. . . . One day we caught a good dozen of them out this way. We put them in a sack, circled back to school, and snuck inside through the basement. Then up we went to our classroom and put them in the top drawer of Miss Holmstead's desk. . . . Next day, when she pulled out the drawer to get her attendance book, out jump a few toads. One lands directly on her bosom, I swear to God. . . . She kept the entire class after school waiting for somebody to confess, but Reggie and I didn't budge. . . . But I couldn't keep my mouth shut on the playground, had to brag about it, and that was my undoing. . . . I had to stay after school every day for a month. Reggie, of course, got away scott-free.

This story, in turn, opened the door to several more "Reggie" stories that would have been forgotten had that toad not leapt onto the sidewalk from out of the past.

Directing the Movie of Your Life

"Sentimental Journeys" offer you a unique opportunity to dramatically re-create a few well-chosen scenes from your life. Returning, say, to the neighborhood library of your youth, you can almost see yourself standing on the front steps some fifty years ago, and so, as you tell your story, you find that you want to get your listeners to "see" you there too. One effective device is to tell your story in the present tense, as if it were happening now. For example: "That's me, standing over there on the top step in my blue gingham dress, my books in the green book bag my father bought me in Cambridge."

Some elders have found it natural and easy to act out their recollected scenes on location. For example, a section of the above-cited "toad" story was acted out in dialogue by its teller. Here are a couple of lines taken verbatim off the videotape his grandson made of the tale:

"What if we get caught?" I say to Reggie.
Well, Reggie—he always walked like this with his hands in his pockets and his head hunched over to one side—Reggie says, "Nobody gets caught unless they want to get caught. And that goes for toads too."

There is another way to dramatically re-create scenes from your past on these Sentimental Journeys: by assigning parts to members of your family. When one elder I know was telling her life stories "on location," her daughter, granddaughters, and great-granddaughter experimented with this technique, taking turns "playing" Grandma at various stages of her life while Grandma herself directed, telling her stand-ins how to act, what to say, and how to say it. It didn't always work. But when it did, as when young Sally portrayed her great-grandmother dancing among the wildflowers, it was breathtaking. As Sally dances, the viewer-listener can hear Grandma's voice over the image:

I loved to dance as a girl, especially out-of-doors in my bare feet. I'd spin around so fast until I'd have to fall down, and then I'd look up at the sky and watch the world spin around me. . . . When you are a little girl, it is easy to imagine that you are at the center of the universe.

Of course, many elders and their families would find directing and improvising scenes too demanding or self-conscious-making. So be it. I simply offer this as an interesting option that has worked for some families. And I can add this: Being "on location" in the landmarks of your past has proved liberating in so many surprising ways that you may find yourself wanting to experiment with new ways to tell your stories. These trips not only energize your memory, they can energize your imagination as well.

Recording Your Journey

More than any other Elder Tale sessions, these trips cry out to be recorded on video both for family members who could not accompany you on your journey and for posterity. Sentimental Journeys can benefit from more elaborate video techniques that take in the details of locale as well as the tale-teller and his listeners.

But I would also advise keeping a journal on this trip.

So many impressions, feelings, and dreams will come rushing at you, you will want to hold on to them to review and think about later. Set aside some time at the end of each day of your journey to set these impressions down in your journal. Among other uses, this journal will become the source of many stories in the future.

Questions, Answers, and Celebrations

You can count on flurries of questions on your Sentimental Journey—"Where did you sit, Grandma?" "What were you wearing?" Being on location stimulates your listeners' appetite for details; seeing part of the picture, they yearn to fill it all in. And on these trips, it is often more difficult to make your listeners wait for a question-and-answer period at the end of all your stories. But, as always, the eagerness of the questioners must be balanced against the need of the tale-teller to maintain the flow of her story.

As for the celebration at the end of your Tale-Telling session, picnics on old landmark spots and dinners at once-familiar diners and restaurants seem to be the favorite ways of the Sentimental Journeyers I know.

Elder Tale X: *Questions You Never Asked/Stories I Never Told*

W e end the Elder Tale Program where we began: with fundamental curiosity about your life.

LISTENERS: Now is the time to ask those special questions that, for whatever reason, you have not asked the elder until now.

ELDERS: Now is the time to tell those special stories that, for whatever reason, you have not told until now. These stories can be about you, your parents and grandparents, or your children or grandchildren, or anyone else who comes to mind.

There are probably a variety of reasons why these questions have not been asked and these stories not told up until now: Perhaps they didn't fit easily into any of the formats that you've been offered above. Or maybe you just ran out of time at the particular session when you were going to ask/tell them. But most likely, the reasons these questions haven't been asked and these stories have not been told is that you weren't emotionally ready for them until now. It took familiarizing yourself with the process of working with your memory and imagination, of digging layer by layer down to the core stories of your life, to prepare yourself for these last questions and stories. Now most of you are not only comfortable satisfying your family's curiosity about your life, but you have experienced the sweet satisfaction of revealing yourself through the stories of a lifetime.

For the Listeners: Questions You Never Asked

Here are a few questions that remained unasked in some families until this last session:

Is there anyone you ever hated bitterly but never told a soul about? /Is there anyone you ever loved passionately but never told a soul about?

What is the most outrageous thing you've ever done?

Did you ever steal anything?

Do you remember ever wishing that you'd been born into another family? (And do you think your parents ever knew your wish?)

As a child, did you ever promise yourself to be a different kind of parent from your own? (Do you think you succeeded?)

Is there any book you read, play you saw, art you viewed, or music you heard that changed your life?

Do you remember any period or moment of your life when you felt more alive than ever before?

If there was one family tradition that you could be assured would be passed on to us and our children and our children's children, what would it be?

If there was only one message, lesson, or bit of wisdom you could pass on to future generations, what would it be?

If you had everything in your life to do over again, what would you do differently?

And this one asked by a minister's daughter:

Have you ever wavered in your belief of God?

There are hundreds of questions that you, the listener, may want to ask at this point. The above are just a sampling of those that have been asked in various families at this session. Frankly, I hesitated before offering them as ex-

amples because I know how easy it is to latch on to someone else's questions instead of digging deeply into yourself
for your own.

But this I can offer: Now is a perfect time to be shame-
lessly egotistical—to try to satisfy those long-burning curi-
osities about how you have figured in the elder's life.
Whatever your question, you may want to share with everyone why it is important to you—what it comes out of in
your own life. To this end, tell your own stories, the stories
that make your questions compelling.

Here's how one high-school–age grandchild introduced
his question at this session:

*I've never told anybody here about this, but one day last
year I skipped school and took the bus into [the city] by myself. I spent the whole day in the streets, just wandering around.
. . . . I didn't talk to anybody, just looked around at people my
age and wondered what my life would be like if I lived there. I
had a ball. Just being on my own and nobody knowing where
I was gave me a terrific feeling, like I was walking around
inside my own movie. . . . And I was wondering, Grandpa,
do you remember ever doing anything like that?*

Grandpa laughed. Indeed, he did remember doing
something like that. And the story with which he responded—about staying an extra day in a strange city after
his business there was concluded—described many of the
same feelings of adventure, self-sufficiency, and aliveness that
his grandson had experienced. The story spoke directly to
the young man. A connection was made across generations,
a sense of continuity in the way they experienced themselves, and by all accounts, it strongly affected both of them.

"The boy's a lot like me," the grandfather commented
to me later with wonder and pride. Then he laughed. "God
help him."

Here's how a daughter-in-law prefaced her question:

*My father used to give us what he called "not-your-birth-
day" presents. Little gifts he'd pull out of his briefcase when*

he came home from work, usually on a Friday night, but not every Friday. He'd pull it out and say, "Well, congratulations, I hear it's not your birthday today." They were very small, these gifts—a comic book, a gold-colored thimble—but I treasured them much more than the big gifts I got on my birthday. . . . Do you remember any special gifts you treasured when you were a child?

Again, this story elicited some wonderful stories that somehow had not been told until now.

And here's how a son posed a question that, at the beginning of the Elder Tale Program, he never could have imagined himself asking:

This past year I've lost two colleagues who were about my age, one to a heart attack, the other to cancer. . . . It's so scary, sometimes I wake up in a sweat thinking about it, that it could happen to me. . . . And I was wondering, does it get any easier as you get older? I mean, can you actually think about death now yourself?

His eighty-two-year-old father's response—beginning with, "Sometimes I think Death is more afraid of me than I am of it"—was funny, touching, relieving, and remarkably instructive by turns. This elder spoke at length about his first encounters with death as a soldier in the Second World War, about dreams he'd had about death and about a book he'd read—*Siddhartha* by Hermann Hesse—that changed the way he thought about it. And finally, he spoke about how telling his stories to his family this past year had made the prospect of his death more acceptable:

God knows, I'd like to go on living forever, but given the way Nature works, I can't complain. . . . I'd hate to have died before my life was over, if you know what I mean. Before I'd raised my family or finished the work I'd set out to do. And now I know I'd hate to have died before I'd done this too: told my stories. Summed it all up.

This session, then, is an *exchange* of stories, a *swapping* of personal experiences and feelings. And, fittingly, it introduces the role of storyteller to the next generations, an important step in the reinvention of this family ritual.

Preparation

The listener starts with his question and then searches in himself for the reasons and personal stories that make his question so important to him. Then he presents his question to the elder *in private* in order to find out if the elder is willing to answer it in front of the whole family. If not, so be it. If he is willing (and, heaven knows, at this point in the program few elders are still holding on to secrets), he now has time to think about and prepare his answer—to find his own stories that match his questioner's.

For the Elders: Stories I Never Told

Some are skeletons that have been clanking around in your closet for so long that you just want to finally let them out:

The story of the time you were fired from your job.

The story of the time you got so drunk you had an accident and had to spend the night in jail.

Some are so shadowy that you cannot be sure if they really happened to you or if they came out of a dream or a family myth, yet they have the power and feel of a core story:

The time you sat on the rooftop of your house through the entire night waiting for your father to come home from a trip.

The story of the moment in a train station when, looking out at the train next to you, you were sure you saw your double looking back at you.

And there was this story, kept secret for years, yet cried to be told:

It was in the middle of June after the Second World War, a very hot, humid afternoon, and we decided to go down to this sheltered bay on the lake [Champlain] to cool off. . . . There was a picnic table, Ricky [my son] was throwing rocks, Thelma [my daughter] was wandering around, and I was crocheting, working on a handbag. Ricky said, "Look at that. What's that in the lake?" The lake was really high that year, kind of wild-looking. The water was perfectly still, just like glass, and in the bay, quite close to us, was a barrel shape. It was black—greenish black—and it looked like it was submerged under water, and had some length to it, maybe ten or fifteen feet, and about three feet across. As I looked at it, it started to move, and Ricky and I stood there, astonished, and then Thelma came over too. We watched this shape move slowly across the bay. Then it picked up speed, and it left a V-shaped wake. We were very quiet, and it didn't make any noise. We looked at each other, trying to figure out what it could possibly be. Then we could see the lake sort of foaming, frothing. Ricky said, "I see a head or something." . . . As it came towards us, it was utterly amazing. It raised up its head. We could see a creature. It looked the way a prehistoric dinosaur would have looked. His head came up like a periscope, maybe three or four feet in the air, and the thing that was utterly amazing was his head, emerald green and curved like a snake. And he just looked at us for a short time, and then just as slowly the head sank down into the lake, and it quietly went away. . . .

To this day, I think of it as an awe-inspiring event, sort of magical, mystical, and special. . . . I don't know what would have happened if we had told people then, if you gave credence to that. Someone would hunt him down for sure, scientists would be interested and sportsmen. I was afraid this beautiful creature would be killed, so we all decided to keep it a secret. . . . And we have, all these years.

Some are stories that have only surfaced in your memory recently. But most are stories that you've been thinking about for some time, yet only now are you emotionally prepared to tell:

The story of the time you almost walked out on your marriage.

The story of the time you thought of ending your life.

The story of the time you heard the voice of your long-dead grandfather speak to you from "the Other Side."

The story of the time you sat on the stairs and watched, transfixed and helpless, as your uncle beat up his wife.

These are the stories you've never told before yet you need to tell now to make the record complete. Like a painter's final touches, these stories give your self-portrait depth; they highlight your individuality.

Prepare for these as you would for any other stories, with "crib notes" and any supporting materials—photographs, news clippings, letters.

Like Telegrams and Epitaphs, Questions You Never Asked/Stories I Never Told go together naturally in a session. But for most of you, a single session will not be sufficient to get to all these stories. You'll probably need another "Question/Story" session, and maybe another after that. In fact, a reprise of this and other sessions has become an annual event in many families—they don't want the stories to stop. And why should they? Once the Elder Tale tradition begins, it develops a life of its own. There are always more stories to tell, more questions to ask, and more wisdom to pass along.

On the last day of that first summer that my mother shared her life stories with my family, she told a story that she had not been ready to tell until that moment. It was about her own mother's death:

When my mother died, I became sick with grief. She had been my sole support after a painful divorce. I cried for days on end. You were only four, Robi, and very worried about me. *"Will you die too?" you asked me. And I picked you up and said, "No, Son, I plan to keep on living as long as you need me."*

She has kept her word.

APPENDIX: *Life-Story Literature*

O bviously, the books and films recommended below are entirely subjective choices. They represent those that have had special meaning and poignancy for me and others while working on our life stories. I intend the list simply as a place for you to begin browsing for your own resources and inspirations.

Seeing Your Life As Stories

Zinsser, William, ed. *Inventing the Truth: The Art and Craft of Memoir*. Boston: Houghton Mifflin, 1987.

This slim volume originated as a series of lectures by the writers Annie Dillard, Toni Morrison, Russell Baker, Alfred Kazin, and Lewis Thomas. It is probably the most instructive book I can commend to anyone interested in collecting her own life stories. These writers' personal observations about the process demonstrate quite clearly that the problems and delights of "reinventing the past" are the same whether we are sitting behind a typewriter or sitting at the center of a family circle.

Welty, Eudora. *One Writer's Beginnings*. Cambridge, MA: Harvard University Press, 1984.

When the novelist Eudora Welty was invited to Harvard to lecture on the art of fiction, she recited, instead, these marvelous, and deceptively simple, autobiographical sketches of growing up in her southern family. From these sketches, we witness the author's growing sensitivity and awareness of herself and the world around her. We see how experience becomes the stuff of stories, and that explains more about Ms. Welty's art then any technical lecture possibly could.

Schwartz, Delmore. *"In Dreams Begin Responsibilities," In Dreams Begin Responsibilities and Other Stories.* New York: New Directions, 1978.

In this mesmerizing short story, Delmore Schwartz imagines his parents' courtship as if he were watching it happen on the screen in a movie theater. The effect is dazzling, disturbing, and powerful. The capacity to see one's life as a "movie" can free the imagination in unexpected and wonderful ways; it can expand your idea of a life story. After reading Schwartz, you may find yourself thinking in terms of scenes, snippets of dialogue, angles of view, and focus, as well as of straight story narrative.

Stevens, George, director. *I Remember Mama.* U.S. 1948. RKO. Screenplay by De Witt Bodeen from the play by John Van Druten.

Like *Avalon*, this film version of the American classic, *MAMA'S BANK ACCOUNT*, by Kathryn Forbes, is a chronicle of an immigrant family in simpler times—in this case, Norwegians in turn-of-the-century San Francisco. It treads heavily into sentimentality—Mama's utter goodness can be overbearing at times—but this film, too, is about the making of a storyteller; the eldest daughter, Katrin, sees stories everywhere in the day-to-day struggles of her indigent family.

Greer, Germaine. *Daddy, We Hardly Knew You.* New York: Alfred A. Knopf, 1989.

Because her recently deceased father had been a painfully despondent man who kept the stories of his life shrouded, Germaine Greer embarks on a journey of detection to discover who "Daddy" really was. Her family story is a mystery that she needs to solve. This 1990 memoir poignantly illustrates the universal hunger to know our family stories. Without the stories, we, like Ms. Greer, feel incomplete.

Masters, Edgar Lee. *Spoon River Anthology*. New York: Collier Books, 1962.

Edgar Lee Masters's 1913 classic, a reinterpretation of the Greek anthology, starts with the candid epitaphs of townspeople buried in a midwestern cemetery. These epitaphs catch the essence of their secret lives. There are some people who find this book gloomy, but I still consider it a marvelous resource for understanding the idea of life themes and core stories. Many storytellers have found it particularly instructive when developing Elder Tale VIII of the program "Telegrams and Epitaphs."

Terkel, Studs. *Hard Times: An Oral History of the Great Depression*. New York: Pantheon, 1970.

The Chicago radio interviewer Studs Terkel brought oral history into the popular consciousness with this volume of recorded and transcribed reminiscences. The popularity of the book alone is testament to people's hunger for firsthand accounts of history.

Malle, Louis, director. *My Dinner with André*. U.S. 1981. André Company. Screenplay by Wallace Shawn and André Gregory.

I hesitated before including this movie here. I have good friends who consider it the most impenetrable piece of cinema ever produced. Yet Louis Malle's two-hour dinner-table conversation between two friends with radically different ideas about love, death, and the quest for self-fulfillment is a magnificent tribute to storytelling itself. And it could serve as textbook on how life stories reveal the essential personality of the teller.

Memoirs and Autobiographies

Again, here are a handful of personal selections. I've aimed for variety, illustrations of the widely different ways in which writers have viewed and assembled the stories of their lives.

Twain, Mark. *Roughing It.* New York: New American Library, 1962, and *Life on the Mississippi.* New York: Bantam Books, 1983.

Mark Twain's two volumes of memoirs remain a sheer joy to read. Not only do they charmingly evoke a colorful period of the American past, but they show how taking imaginative license in the telling of a life story creates a truth of its own.

Merton, Thomas. *The Seven Storey Mountain.* New York: Walker, 1985.

Thomas Merton's book is the preeminent modern spiritual autobiography. The most significant events of Merton's life occurred internally—inside his head and heart. There are many clues here for elders preparing for Elder Tale VII of the program, "Epiphanies and Lessons."

Kazin, Alfred. *A Walker in the City.* New York: Harcourt Brace Jovanovich, 1951.

Alfred Kazin's memoir of his youth in New York City tells its stories from the outside in—through his senses. This book demonstrates better than any I know how details of sight, sound, feel, smell, and taste can evoke a personal experience.

Arlen, Michael, Jr. *Exiles* in *Passage to Arat and Exiles.* New York: Penguin, 1982.

Michael Arlen, Jr.'s impressionistic memoir of life with his aristocratic immigrant parents is not only a model of clean, clear writing, but it shows how small incidents in family life can reveal volumes about family relationships.

Dillard, Annie. *An American Childhood.* New York: Harper & Row, 1987.

A whimsical family memoir, Annie Dillard's book contains one of my favorite lines in contemporary American autobiography: "I grew up in Pittsburgh in the 1950s in a house full of comedians, reading books." An excellent antidote to self-seriousness when this life-review business starts to lose its joy.

Wolff, Geoffrey. *The Duke of Deception*. New York: Random House, 1990, and Wolff, Tobias. *This Boy's Life*. New York: Harper & Row, 1990.

A pair of memoirs of devastating childhoods by, respectively, Geoffrey Wolff and Tobias Wolff, brothers and both remarkable writers. Each manages to suffuse his account of dreadful childhood experiences with great affection; much of that affection seems to derive from gratitude for experience itself. A reading of these books has made it easier for some elders to recall and tell difficult stories from their own childhoods.

Saint-Exupéry, Antoine de. *Wind, Sand, And Stars*. New York: Reynal & Hitchcock, 1940.

Antoine de Saint-Exupéry (best known for his children's classic, *The Little Prince*) demonstrates the elegance of simplicity and the magic in details in this memoir of his years as a mail pilot in the early days of aviation.

Miller, Henry. *Tropic of Cancer*. New York: Random House, 1983.

Henry Miller's bawdy reminiscence of bohemian life in New York and Paris is obviously not everybody's cup of tea— many will find its sexual explicitness offensive. But as an object lesson in personal honesty (and the appetite for life that drives that honesty), Miller's books have no equal. Many elders have found the book a liberating reminder of their own passionate youths.

Baker, Russell. *Growing Up*. New York: New American Library, 1983.

The humorist Russell Baker's modest and relentlessly entertaining memoir of his early years proves how very much you can reveal about yourself by focusing your stories not on yourself but on the people around you—most particularly, your parents.

Universal Myths That Shape Our Life Stories

Inspired by Bill Moyers's televised interviews with Joseph Campbell, many of us have begun to rediscover the importance of myth in our lives. No matter what their source—primal societies, ancient Greek and Roman civilization, sacred scriptures, or popular folklore—myths convey the universal themes of our lives. In myths, we find the yearnings, dreams, quests, anxieties, and personal odysseys that connect human beings of all times and all cultures. "We hunger for myths to live by," Campbell said. And as elders, we hunger for myths that can help us interpret our lives and make sense of our stories. What mythic themes run through our own lives? What universal stories are echoed in our own stories?

Campbell, Joseph, and Bill Moyers. *The Power of Myth*. New York: Doubleday, 1988.

"I never met anyone who could better tell a story," Bill Moyers said of the late Joseph Campbell. Whether you view these interviews on videocassette or read them in the book, you cannot help but be bewitched by the way Campbell links, say, a biblical allergory to the movie *Star Wars*, or a Native American legend to a Chinese fable. I know of no more accessible introduction to the world of mythology and its relation to life-story themes.

Eliot, Alexander. *The Universal Myths: Heroes, Gods, Tricksters, and Others*, rev. ed. New York: New American Library, 1990.

This highly readable compendium of world myths by Alexander Eliot is arranged by theme, beginning with tales of creation and moving through stories of magic, lovers, quests, and mortal tests to tales of death and rebirth. It provides a concise and entertaining survey of the range of myths out there. And when you come across myths that seem to resonate with something in your own life, you can go off to the library to find more expanded versions of them.

Amoss, Pamela T. and Stevan Harrell, eds. *Other Ways of Growing Old*. Palo Alto: Stanford University Press, 1981.

This collection of anthropological essays offers highly readable firsthand accounts of the role of the elder in a variety of primitive societies. Of special interest to us is its pan-cultural depiction of the elder as a living repository of the myths, rituals, and family stories that hold a society together.

Jung, Carl G. *Memories, Dreams, Reflections*, trans. rev. ed., ed. Aniela Jaffe and Richard and Clara Winston. New York: Pantheon, 1963.

Considered by many to be the intellectual and spiritual father of Campbell, the psychologist Carl Jung devoted most of his career to exploring the universal myths that he believed were the structures of our collective unconscious. For Jung, myths, fantasies, and dreams were all products of the unconscious—the basis of all that is human. None of Jung's books is easy going for the uninitiated, but for those of you who wish to further investigate the psychic origins of myths, this is the basic text. And as we move in our personal investigation from myths to dreams, it seems an appropriate one.

Kazan, Elia, director. *East of Eden*. U.S. 1955. Warner. Screenplay by Paul Osborn from the novel by John Steinbeck.

One of the most familiar and, in many ways, most complex myths in our culture is the biblical account of the brothers Cain and Abel. That story covers a great deal of primary territory: forgiveness and unforgiveness, loyalty and betrayal, love and rejection, pride and humility. In his monumental novel *East of Eden*, John Steinbeck reinterpreted this myth as an American family saga, keeping most of its basic themes intact, and in 1960, the director Elia Kazan re-created Steinbeck's book as a marvelous film. Watching the film, it is easy to understand how myths transcend a particular time or place; it is possible to glimpse the idea that our life stories are the stories of Everyman.

PHOTOGRAPH CREDITS

The pictures reproduced here are used by courtesy of families who participated in the development of the Elder Tale Program except for the following:

Library of Congress Prints and Photographs Division
Pages 26, 58, 122, 134, 144, 150, 162, 184, 196, 218

The Museum of Modern Art
Pages 44, 52, 98, 110

Smithsonian Institution / National Anthropological Archives
Page 28

National Archives Still Photo Branch
Page 176

Northfield / Mount Hermon School—Dolben Library Archives
Page 206

About the Authors

ROBERT U. AKERET, ED.D., received his doctorate in psychology from Columbia University and his certificate in psychoanalysis from the William Alanson White Institute. A past president of the Association of Psychoanalytic Psychologists, he is the author of two previous books, *Not by Words Alone*, a professional memoir, and *Photoanalysis*, on analyzing photographs for psychological meaning. Dr. Akeret has practiced psychoanalysis in New York City for thirty years. He also lectures and conducts workshops on the gathering and sharing of Elder Tales.

DANIEL KLEIN is a graduate of Harvard and the author of nine books.